The Entrepreneur's Complete Self-Assessment Guide

The Entrepreneur's Complete Self-Assessment Guide

How to Determine Your Potential for Success

Douglas A Gray

Kogan
Page

To Diana, my wife, partner, and favourite entrepreneur

First published in Canada in 1986 by
International Self-Counsel Press Ltd,
306 West 25th Street, North Vancouver,
British Columbia V7N 2GI.

Copyright © International Self-Counsel Press Ltd 1986

This edition first published in Great
Britain in 1987 by Kogan Page Ltd,
120 Pentonville Road, London N1 9JN.

New material copyright © Kogan Page Ltd 1987

British Library Cataloguing in Publication Data

Gray, Douglas A.
    The entrepreneur's complete self-
    assessment guide: how to determine your
    potential for success.
    1. Success in business
    I. Title
    650.1   HF5386

    ISBN 1-85091-454-0
            1-85091-310-2 Pbk

Printed and bound in Great Britain
by Billing & Sons Limited, Worcester.

Contents

Part 3: Setting Up

Introduction

This book is written for the aspiring small business entrepreneur. This includes anyone who is considering self-employment, either part-time or full-time. Experienced entrepreneurs should also find this book very helpful. Practical step-by-step checklists, quizzes, tips, and techniques are provided to help you assess yourself as a potential entrepreneur, and guide you through the first stages of starting your own business.

In the past decade, the number of people starting their own businesses has increased significantly. VAT registrations increased by 10.8 per cent between 1979 and 1984, and these represent only those businesses which exceed the VAT turnover threshold.

Many people fantasise about being self-employed at some point in their life. For most people the dream never comes true. The fear of taking a risk and uncertainty about the future prevent most dreams from developing.

This guide is designed to encourage you to consider the many exciting aspects of starting a business and to view the causes of small business failure in better perspective. The personal biography section and the quizzes will help you assess your strengths and weaknesses. The chapters on finding and evaluating business opportunities and sources of finance should stimulate your creative imagination. The checklists will act as a practical reminder of the questions that you must answer before you decide to commit your time and money to an entrepreneurial venture. In short, by the time you have completed this book, you will have had a dry run of the critical business considerations that can make the difference between the success and failure of your business idea.

Work through the chapters, quizzes and checklists sequentially. You may find it helpful to buy a three-ring binder and lined paper to organise your detailed responses and the ideas that spring from them.

This book is based on extensive research of the existing literature on small business management and entrepreneurship: in-depth interviews with thousands of successful and unsuccessful entrepreneurs; personal experience based on seven successful business start-ups; experience as a business lawyer; and consultation with business advisers, including solicitors, accountants, small business consultants and counsellors, business transfer agents, economic development officials, commercial lending managers, and venture capital investors.

Small business entrepreneurs play a vital role in the economy. Their spirit, ingenuity and enthusiasm make our society dynamic, and provide employment opportunities, economic growth, greater efficiency through competition, and the creation of new products and services.

The information in this book will help you decide if you want to be self-employed. If you do decide to embark on your own venture, this book will help you become a successful entrepreneur.

Note. This book attempts to highlight business concepts and techniques accurately. However, the information is general in nature and if legal or other expert advice is required, you should obtain the services of competent professionals.

Part 1
So You Want to Be an Entrepreneur?

Chapter 1

Entrepreneurs – Who Are They?

What is an entrepreneur?

An entrepreneur is one who organises, manages, and assumes the risks of a business or enterprise. This simple but encompassing statement could include anyone who runs a small, medium, or large business. It could include an independent operator, or the entrepreneur who works as part of a team or in a partnership.

Another definition of an entrepreneur is someone who exhibits entrepreneurial characteristics. The most common characteristics of entrepreneurs are detailed in Chapter 3.

The motives of the entrepreneur are many: the desire for independence; the opportunity for achievement; the need to avoid unemployment; and the drive to meet personal, emotional, psychological, and financial needs. (These motives do not necessarily translate into achieving great wealth.)

Types of entrepreneur

There are many different types of entrepreneur, each distinguishable by the manner in which they operate.

Read through the following descriptions of entrepreneurial styles. Ask yourself which type you prefer and why. Then write your thoughts down to use as a reference point from which you can explore your preferences. Which type of entrepreneur do you think you want to be?

1. Soloist

A soloist is a self-employed individual who operates either

alone or with a few employees only. Soloists include tradespeople, brokers, small family businesses, and so on.

2. Key partner

A key partner is an individual in partnership with others, but the partners are either inactive or they assume a minor role. A key partner is like a soloist; he or she is a person who needs a lot of personal autonomy, but requires partners for financial support.

3. Grouper

These are individuals who prefer the psychological and/or financial relief of working with a group of partners. They are less autonomous than key partners as decisions are shared by the group. Medium to large legal and accounting firms are good examples of where this type of entrepreneur can be found.

4. Professional

This category includes traditional professionals such as solicitors, accountants, dentists, doctors, architects, and engineers. Consultants can also be included in this group. These self-employed experts are highly specialised and have had considerable higher education. The consultants may or may not have advanced education, but they do have very clear and marketable expertise. Professionals generally do not perceive themselves as entrepreneurs, but they do have the entrepreneurial traits required to survive and succeed.

5. Inventor-researcher

Inventor-researchers are usually tinkerers or frustrated professionals who decide to start another business, such as a laboratory to test a new product or service. They generally have good ideas, but frequently lack managerial skill. They can also become emotionally involved with pet projects, or enjoy the challenge of discovery without focusing on the practical market applications.

A variation of the inventor-researcher is the creative innovator who has ideas for better products, perceives the market need, then creates a company to develop, manufacture, and sell the product.

14

6. High-tech

A high-tech entrepreneur generally has advanced education, and technical expertise, particularly with electronics or computers. He or she may have the capacity to assimilate complex concepts, is generally competitive, and enjoys the challenge of being on the leading edge of new technological developments.

7. Work force builder

An individual who starts working on his or her own, then builds a large company through astute hiring, delegation, and organisational abilities, is a work force builder. The carpenter who works individually, gradually quotes for larger jobs subcontracting as required, and ends up with a large shopfitting firm, is an example of a work force builder.

8. Inveterate initiator

This person enjoys the challenge of initiating new enterprises, but quickly loses interest in maintaining them once the challenge has been met. The inveterate initiator is frequently looking for opportunities to start new enterprises. He or she usually sells the existing business and uses the proceeds to start the next. Generally this type of person goes into business with the specific goal of selling it for profit.

9. Concept multiplier

This type of individual recognises a successful business concept that has the potential to be duplicated with additional profit. Franchising is one concept multiplier approach; another is licensing; another still is chain expansion.

10. Acquirer

This person prefers to take over an existing business rather than start a new one. That way the risk is reduced because there is established goodwill. A lot of the difficulties and struggles experienced in the initial years are eliminated, allowing energy to be directed to increasing profit and enhancing business growth.

11. Speculator

Many speculators have found their fortune in property. This can take many forms: buying rented residential property, upgrading the premises, increasing the rent and then selling it; buying and renovating houses for profit; or subdividing land, thereby increasing its value. Land provides the leverage to allow you collateral to borrow against. This type of entrepreneur has the potential to acquire enormous assets on which capital gains can be earned. Other commodities, such as antiques, art, and stamps can also provide a profitable business return.

12. Turn-about artist

The turn-about artist buys companies with problems, but potential for profit. He or she first identifies the areas of weakness in the business, and makes a low offer. The entrepreneur then reduces costs and payrolls to eliminate losses, removes unprofitable lines, and adds more promising ones. Generally he or she makes the company a lean, efficient business. The business is then sold at a profit.

13. Value manipulator

A value manipulator is an entrepreneur who acquires an asset at a low price, then legally manipulates the financial structure so that it appears to be worth a lot more. It can then be resold at a higher price. For example, if a company balance sheet shows an unfavourable current ratio and you persuade creditors to accept longer term notes on the debt, the current ratio would be suddenly much larger, which would result in a higher resale value.

14. Lifestyle entrepreneur

An individual who enjoys the fringe benefits of success and looks on a business as a means to attain the trappings of the 'good life' can be considered a lifestyle entrepreneur. This type of person is not interested in any business that might involve personnel or growth problems, or extensive financial or time commitments. The primary interest is consistent cash flow. Therefore this individual seeks a business that commonly involves putting together deals, acting as the middleman.

Normally, the success of the lifestyle entrepreneur is attributable to the numerous contacts he or she has in a specialised branch of industry.

15. Committed manager

The committed manager looks on his or her business as lifetime employment to be nurtured and developed at every stage, from start-up to profitability. Personal satisfaction comes from the challenge of directing the growing concern and managing all its changing problems.

Some committed managers have qualities of the inveterate initiator. On one hand, the entrepreneur starts a company intending to sell it for a profit in the future so that the money can go into new ventures. On the other hand, the entrepreneur may be tempted to sell the business but stay on as the manager for the satisfaction of watching the company grow. But this type of person can function successfully only if he or she is completely autonomous. Sharing authority with or receiving direction from someone else is generally an unworkable relationship and will not last long for this type of person.

16. Conglomerator

This is the kind of entrepreneur who obtains control of one company, then uses shares of that company to buy control of other businesses, thereby creating a conglomerate. One common technique is to buy companies with lower price-earnings ratios through the parent company. The new acquisition's price-earnings ratio will generally increase after merging with the parent company, as will the overall conglomerate stock value.

17. Capital aggregator

The capital aggregator has the capacity to raise large sums of money, through investors or otherwise, then acquire very attractive businesses through extensive financial leverage.

18. Matriarch or patriarch

A matriarch or patriarch is an individual who heads a family-owned business. His or her desire is to continue to have family members control the business, whether the company is privately held or publicly quoted.

19. Going public

Some entrepreneurs start or acquire a company with the sole intention of taking the company public. This means the company sells its shares on the Unlisted Securities Market or the Stock Exchange; private investors can sell their stake in part or in full, and achieve a substantial profit on their investments.

Starting up as an entrepreneur

A person may choose to become an entrepreneur at any stage of life. The following examples are meant to stimulate your ideas about when to start up a business. Also they may give you ideas to initiate ventures with other people who are considering starting a business, but have not yet decided to embark.

It is possible to start an entrepreneurial venture from virtually any point. Entrepreneurs start new ventures while at school or college, after leaving school, during times of unemployment, from the home, or from existing businesses. Think of these possibilities as starting points:

(a) Part-time at school
(b) Part-time at college, targeting the off- or on-campus markets
(c) For college course work or thesis study
(d) After dropping out of college
(e) After graduating with a developed business plan
(f) After resigning from a job, or after being dismissed or laid off
(g) After retirement
(h) After leaving a job, but with advance preparation for a business venture completed while still employed either as a natural outcome from job-related duties and contracts or completely unrelated to previous job duties
(i) After moonlighting with part-time business at weekends or in the evenings
(j) After business operated from the home succeeds

(k) By an established entrepreneur, either in a similar or unrelated industry.

Now that you have considered some of the starting points to self-employment, write down which categories fit your situation.

Chapter 2

Do You Have What It Takes?

Most people start a business without ever completing a thorough, honest appraisal of themselves and their personal, family, and business needs and goals. Without this appraisal, the potential to succeed in business is very limited.

This chapter is designed to assist you to focus on your strong points, identify your weaknesses, and deal with areas that need improvement. Most people have never completed this type of exercise; you will gain a competitive edge because you have done so.

Expand as fully as you like to the questions under each different heading. Take all the time necessary. Use extra paper if required. It is important to be free from distractions to obtain the optimum benefit.

Autobiography

Summarise your own biography. Review in detail all facets of your past, including work positions, projects you have undertaken, education, credentials you have earned, free-time activities including hobbies and sports, and family and personal relationships. Include all your work experiences during summers, weekends or holidays. Start with your current achievements and work backwards.

Skill

Refer to Figure 2.1, which lists various skills. Circle the 10 skills that you are best at and enjoy the most. If you have skills not listed, add them on.

achieving	enforcing	learning	retrieving
acting	establishing	lecturing	reviewing
adapting	estimating	listening	risking
administering	evaluating	managing	scheduling
advising	examining	manipulating	selecting
analysing	expanding	memorising	selling
arbitrating	experimenting	mediating	sewing
arranging	explaining	modelling	sharing
assembling	extracting	motivating	singing
assessing	filing	navigating	sketching
auditing	financing	negotiating	sorting
budgeting	fixing	observing	speaking
building	following	organising	studying
calculating	formulating	painting	summarising
charting	founding	performing	supervising
checking	gathering	persuading	supplying
classifying	generating	photographing	symbolising
coaching	giving	piloting	synthesising
communicating	guiding	planning	systemising
compiling	handling	predicting	taking instructions
composing	heading	preparing	talking
computing	helping	presenting	teaching
conceptualizing	hypothesising	printing	team-building
conducting	identifying	problem-solving	testing & proving
consolidating	illustrating	producing	training
constructing	imagining	programming	transcribing
controlling	implementing	projecting	translating
coordinating	improving	promoting	trouble-shooting
counselling	improvising	proof-reading	tutoring
creating	increasing	publicising	typing
deciding	influencing	purchasing	umpiring
defining	informing	questioning	uncovering
delivering	initiating	reading	understanding
designing	innovating	reasoning	unifying
detailing	inspecting	recommending	upgrading
diagnosing	inspiring	recording	using
directing	installing	recruiting	winning
displaying	integrating	referring	working
dissecting	interpreting	rehabilitating	writing
distributing	interviewing	repairing	Other:
diverting	inventing	reporting	
dramatising	inventorying	representing	
drawing	investigating	researching	
driving	judging	resolving	
editing	leading	restoring	

Figure 2.1. *Skill areas*

Personality

Refer to Figure 2.2, which lists various personality attributes. If you have attributes not listed, add them. Tick each attribute that you believe you possess. Now circle the ten attributes that you believe are your strongest and of which you are the most proud.

Accomplishments

1. Non-job-related

List your most significant *non-job-related* accomplishments. Be specific and go back as far as possible (eg running a marathon, acting as manager for a college pop group, building your own tree house when you were age 11). List as many events as possible that are important to you.

1. _____
2. _____
3. _____
4. _____
5. _____
6. _____
7. _____
8. _____
9. _____
10. _____

In the right-hand margin, rank the accomplishments you have listed from the most important to the least important. Then, using the list on page 24, write down all the specific skills, talents, and attributes needed to accomplish each task. (*Skills* are things that you can do: developed or acquired abilities such as instructing, administering, and problem-solving. *Attributes* are characteristics of a person, such as an analytical or enquiring mind. *Talents* are natural endowment: often a unique gift or special, creative attribute.)

accurate	deliberate	ingenious	respectful
active	democratic	inquisitive	responsible
adaptable	dependable	insightful	responsive
adventurous	determined	intellectual	secure
affable	dignified	intelligent	self-assured
affectionate	diligent	kind	self-aware
aggressive	disciplined	lighthearted	self-confident
agreeable	discreet	likeable	self-controlled
alert	dominant	logical	self-directed
ambitious	eager	loyal	self-reliant
amicable	easygoing	mature	self-starting
analytical	economical	methodical	sensible
animated	effective	meticulous	sensitive
articulate	effervescent	modest	serene
artistic	efficient	motivated	serious
assertive	emotional	natural	sincere
attentive	encouraging	neat	sociable
attractive	energetic	nurturing	stable
bold	enterprising	objective	strong
broad-minded	enthusiastic	obliging	sympathetic
businesslike	ethical	observant	systematic
calm	exacting	optimistic	tactful
capable	fair-minded	organised	talented
caring	faithful	original	teachable
cautious	farsighted	patient	tenacious
charming	firm	perceptive	thorough
cheerful	flexible	persistent	thoughtful
clearsighted	forceful	persuasive	tough
compassionate	formal	poised	trusting
competent	frank	polite	trustworthy
competitive	friendly	positive	unaffected
concise	generous	practical	unassuming
confident	gentle	precise	understanding
congenial	goal oriented	productive	unexcitable
conscientious	helpful	prudent	uninhibited
conservative	honest	punctual	unselfish
considerate	honourable	purposeful	versatile
consistent	hopeful	quick	warm
constructive	humane	rational	well-groomed
cooperative	humanistic	realistic	wholesome
cosmopolitan	humorous	reasonable	wise
courageous	idealistic	reflective	witty
creative	imaginative	relaxed	Other:
curious	independent	reliable	
daring	industrious	reserved	
decisive	informal	resourceful	

Figure 2.2. *Personality attributes*

	Task	Skills used	Attributes demonstrated	Talents shown
1.				
2.				
3.				
4.				
5.				
6.				
7.				
8.				
9.				
10.				

2. Job-related

List the most significant *job-related* accomplishments in your life. Be specific and go back as far as possible. Include any part-time or full-time work, summer jobs, or weekend jobs (eg coordinating a major conference, winning the best employee contest at a fast-food restaurant, negotiating a major contract for your employer). List as many events as possible that are important to you.

1. _____
2. _____
3. _____
4. _____
5. _____
6. _____
7. _____
8. _____
9. _____
10. _____

In the right-hand margin, rank the accomplishments you have listed from the most important to the least important. Again, using the list on page 25, write down all the specific skills, talents, and attributes needed to accomplish each task.

	Task	Skills used	Attributes demonstrated	Talents shown
1.				
2.				
3.				
4.				
5.				
6.				
7.				
8.				
9.				
10.				

3. Skills profile

The next step is to fill in the skills profile graph shown below. On the left-hand side of the graph, list all the skills that you have identified in sections 1 and 2 above. Next, add up the number of times that you have listed each skill and shade in the frequency in the skill column by referring to the numbers at the bottom of the graph. This will give you a good visual demonstration of how important certain skills are in your activities.

Skills profile graph

	List of identified skills	Frequency of use
1.		
2.		
3.		
4.		
5.		
6.		
7.		
8.		
9.		
10.		

List of identified skills	Frequency of use
11. _____	_____
12. _____	_____
13. _____	_____
14. _____	_____
15. _____	_____
16. _____	_____
17. _____	_____
18. _____	_____
19. _____	_____
20. _____	_____

0 1 2 3 4 5 6 7 8 9 10 11 12 13 14 15 16

Personal interests

Imagine that you are reading a magazine, book or newspaper, or watching TV. Which of the following topics interest you? Rank them in order of importance from the most important to the least important:

__Entertainment   __Business   __Science
__Sports   __Politics   __The arts
__Social trends   __Human interest   __Environment
__Finance   __Health   __Other

Do you see your areas of interest in any way bringing you closer to your business idea? How would you describe the top five areas of interest as being relevant to your possible business goals?

_____
_____
_____

Spectator activities

List your spectator activities in order of importance (eg films, sports, theatre, TV):

_____

_____

_____

How do you see these areas of activity assisting you in your business goals?

_____

_____

_____

Recreational activities

List the recreational activities in which you participate in order of importance (eg walking, jogging, tennis, climbing, sailing, cycling, skating, exercise classes, dancing).

_____

_____

_____

How do you see these areas of activity assisting you in your business goals?

_____

_____

_____

Hobbies

List your hobbies in order of importance (eg cooking, photography, reading, gardening, painting).

_____

_____

_____

How do you see these areas of activity assisting you in your business goals?

_____

_____

_____

Social/community activities

List your social/community activities in order of importance (eg parent/teacher association, church or hospital auxiliary, other volunteer organisations or clubs).

_____

_____

_____

How do you see these areas of activity assisting you in your business goals?

_____

_____

_____

Employment

List all the roles you have assumed in your present job or past jobs in order of importance (eg responsibility, authority, budgeting, selling).

_____

_____

_____

How do you see these role areas assisting you in your business goals?

_____

_____

_____

Lifestyle

Think of your own lifestyle and work preferences. List the activities or circumstances in order of importance that provide you with the greatest amount of personal satisfaction and enjoyment — the things you enjoy doing the most (eg travelling, hiking, playing with your children).

_____

_____

_____

Dislikes

Think of the activities or circumstances that you enjoy the least. In order of severity, list the things that cause you the greatest amount of personal anxiety, unhappiness or frustration.

_____

_____

_____

The future

Imagine yourself 20 years from now. Describe what your ideal lifestyle and work style will be like. Consider where you would like to live, who your close friends are likely to be, your income, involvement in family, work, community or religious activities, holiday and recreational lifestyle and material possessions.

_____

_____

_____

Now assume that you have been told you have exactly one year to live from today. You will enjoy good health in the interim, but will not be able to obtain any more life assurance, or borrow any large sums of money for a final fling. Also assume that you could spend that last year of your life doing whatever you want to do. Write down the goals you would want to accomplish if you had one year to live.

_____

_____

_____

The present

Think about your present situation. Consider each of the following areas: marital, family, career, social, financial, spiritual, personal, physical, emotional. List what you perceive to be your strong points and weak points in each category. Once you have done that, reflect on the impact self-employment will have on each of the nine categories.

	Strong points	Weak points	Impact of self-employment
Marital	_____	_____	_____
Family	_____	_____	_____
Career	_____	_____	_____
Social	_____	_____	_____
Financial	_____	_____	_____
Spiritual	_____	_____	_____
Personal	_____	_____	_____
Physical	_____	_____	_____
Emotional	_____	_____	_____

Now ask someone who knows you well (eg spouse, relative, close friend) to list what they consider to be your five strengths and five weaknesses, and rank them. Do others see you as you see yourself? Do you believe their perceptions of you are accurate?

Personal goals

List the personal goals that you wish to attain in one, five, and ten years.

One year: _____
_____

Five years: _____
_____

Ten years: _____
_____

Reactions

If you haven't already, discuss your thoughts of going into business with your spouse, family, relatives, friends and business associates. Describe how they react.

Spouse: _____

Family: _____

Relatives: _____

Friends: _____

Business associates: _____

Dealing with doubt

Refer back to your personal and work-related accomplishments listed on pages 22-4. Describe any doubts you experienced or risks you took before the achievement became a reality.

Doubt or risk	How it was overcome
_____	_____
_____	_____
_____	_____

List five achievements you plan for the future.

_____

_____

_____

_____

_____

Now for each planned achievement, describe any doubts or risks. Devise and summarise contingency plans to deal with these doubts or risks.

Doubt or risk	Contingency plan
_____	_____
_____	_____
_____	_____
_____	_____
_____	_____

31

The experience of others

List any friends, relatives or acquaintances who own and operate their own businesses, including professionals who have a private practice. List their types of business. How do you view them and their self-employed roles? Have you talked to them about how they enjoy their business?

_____

_____

_____

Style

If you have ever worked in a small company, list the things you liked most and least about your experience.

Liked most	Liked least
_____	_____
_____	_____
_____	_____

If you have ever worked for a large company (over 500 employees), list the things you liked most and least about your experience.

Liked most	Liked least
_____	_____
_____	_____
_____	_____

If you have ever worked in your own business (part-time or full-time), list the things you liked most and least about your experience.

Liked most	Liked least
_____	_____
_____	_____
_____	_____

The bottom line

What are your reasons for wanting to go into business for yourself?

_____

_____

_____

_____

Make a list of the external influences that bear, or might bear, upon your success or failure in business (eg increase in interest rates, problems with suppliers, competition, illness).

_____

_____

_____

_____

Think of all the businesses you can, and assume that you could go into whichever business you wished. Make a list of the ten businesses you most definitely would want to enter. Rank your answers in order of preference.

1. _____   6. _____

2. _____   7. _____

3. _____   8. _____

4. _____   9. _____

5. _____   10. _____

Why did you find the top three choices most attractive?

_____

_____

_____

_____

Chapter 3

Common Characteristics of Entrepreneurs

What kind of person becomes an entrepreneur? What characteristics must a successful entrepreneur have? Are you born with these entrepreneurial traits or can they be learned?

This chapter discusses the 44 most common characteristics of successful entrepreneurs. These are traits that entrepreneurs, venture capitalists, psychologists, and academics believe to be important to achieve entrepreneurial success. It is highly unlikely that any one person is exceptionally strong or weak in all of these categories. They are a guide only. As you read through this chapter, think how these characteristics relate to your life.

1. Continuous goal-setting

Ability to set clear goals that are challenging but attainable; ability continually to re-evaluate and adjust goals to make sure they are consistent with your interests, talents, and values, as well as your personal or business needs. Rather than being content with reaching goals, successful entrepreneurs continually set new goals to challenge themselves.

2. Perseverance

Steadfast pursuit of an aim; constant persistence; continuing to strive for a goal despite temporary obstacles; strong determination to reach goals regardless of personal sacrifice.

3. Business knowledge

The entrepreneur must understand basic principles by which a business survives and prospers. That means comprehending the roles management, partners, and employees must perform to maintain a viable business. Although the entrepreneur must be in control of overall goals, he or she cannot perform each task without help. Awareness of the function of personnel in marketing, accounting, tax, financing, planning and management, and how to deal with them, is therefore required.

If a prospective entrepreneur is bored or baffled by the administrative side of business, he or she is not likely to be successful. An alternative is to find a trusted partner who has the aptitudes described.

4. Dealing with failure

Disappointed but not discouraged by failure; ability to use failures as learning experiences, so that similar problems can be avoided in the future; attitude that setbacks are only temporary barriers to your goals; strong capacity to build on success.

5. Self-determination

Belief that you control your success or failure, and that it is not decided by luck, circumstance, or external events; belief in self-determined destinies and that you have the ability to achieve the goals you have set.

6. Moderate risk-taking

Ability to identify risks and weigh their relative dangers; preference for taking calculated risks to achieve goals that are high but realistic. Risks are moderate, contrary to the stereotype that entrepreneurs are gamblers or high risk takers.

7. Persistent problem-solving

Ability to resolve problems effectively and resourcefully; determination to look on problems as challenges; capacity to deal repeatedly with a multitude of such challenges, showing willingness and tenacity. Desire to pay attention to detail, and obtain all the information required to test solutions, so that the best one is attained.

8. Initiative

Self-reliant nature; desire and willingness to initiate action without needing or taking direction from others; ability to solve problems, fill a vacuum or lead others when the need exists; attracted to situations where your impact on problems can be measured. Entrepreneurs perceive themselves as strong, capable, and in control, which allows them to be innovative and creative in expressing their ideas; entrepreneurs are active individuals who want to work on their idea immediately so that they can see results at once.

9. Drive and energy level

A high level of stamina is important to meet the intense demands of running a business; ability to work hard for long hours with less sleep than normal is essential; prepared to make personal sacrifices in order to reach objectives successfully; single-mindedness until your goal is reached.

10. Willingness to consult experts

Desire to seek the assistance of others when it is required to accomplish your goals; entrepreneurs often work alone, and can become so independent that they request help from no one; successful entrepreneurs avoid that trap.

11. Physical health

Staying healthy is essential to the intense demands and ongoing pressures of your own business, especially during its early years. If you are ill, there might not be anyone to take over. Even if there is a plan for a temporary manager, that person is unlikely to be as committed or knowledgeable as you. In either case, the effect on the business could be disastrous. Also, remember that there is no paid sick leave for the owner-manager of a business.

12. Mental and emotional health

The long hours and pressures of business demand your emotional well-being. The success of a business may be determined by whether or not your spouse, family, and friends can pull together and provide emotional support and understanding. If your marriage is shaky, or if you are emotionally isolated and unhappy, the extra strain can be intolerable. Any kind of emotional strain that affects the owner-manager's capacity for calm and objective thinking is going to affect the business.

13. Tolerance of uncertainty

Ability to live with the uncertainty of job security; the entrepreneur must face many crises, take risks, and allow for temporary failures without panic; successful entrepreneurs accept uncertainty as an integral part of being in business.

14. Using feedback

The skill to seek and use feedback on personal performance and goals for the business; the skill to take any remedial action required; feedback is requested from employees, the management team, and professional advisers.

15. Competing against self-imposed standards

Tendency to establish realistic standards of performance and to compete with yourself to meet those objectives; a competitive nature naturally manifests itself by competing with others, but the criteria for performance level are internal.

16. Seeking personal responsibility

Wanting control or accepting authority, and therefore being personally responsible for the outcome of events; must genuinely enjoy the challenge of authority; understand and accept personal responsibility.

17. Self-confidence

Strong but realistic belief in yourself and your ability to achieve personal or business goals. Successful entrepreneurs have an enduring faith in themselves that gives them the capacity to recover from a serious defeat or disappointment.

18. Versatility

Capable of dealing effectively with many subjects or tasks at the same time; qualified to assume different roles and switch back and forth as required. During the early stages of the business, the entrepreneur will assume numerous and diverse business responsibilities, including marketing, sales, credit and collection, finances, employee selection, accounting, planning, and negotiating.

19. Desire for independence

Genuine desire to be your own boss, free from external direction and control; a sincere willingness and proven ability to be self-disciplined in sometimes isolated working conditions; ability to organise activities to reach personal goals. Successful entrepreneurs are not usually joiners by nature; they may join only to network, to make business contacts, further their ventures, obtain useful information to solve problems. Studies have shown that reliance on social interaction and friendship inhibits entrepreneurial behaviour.

20. Using positive imagery

The ability to fantasise about goals and objectives is a common characteristic of successful entrepreneurs. The unconscious mind can then be influenced to accept the picture as a reality waiting to happen, which provides motivation and a sense of direction.

21. Sense of purpose

A feeling of mission motivates the entrepreneur to go into business; the entrepreneurial activity has meaning. These factors may be the desire to make an attractive profit, the desire to sell some necessary and unique product or service, or the desire to develop your ideas or skills without the constraints of others' expectations.

22. Objectivity

Ability to distinguish between yourself and the business, so when you make a mistake you have the strength to admit it and take corrective action; desire to deal with issues and decisions rationally and logically rather than emotionally.

23. Achievement-oriented

Desire to take on challenges and test your abilities to the limit. Successful entrepreneurs are not ambivalent about success. They concentrate on ways to succeed, not what will happen if they fail. Because they are objective, though, they build a 'what if' scenario into the business plan, so that they anticipate problems and develop strategies to surmount obstacles in advance. Successful entrepreneurs adopt the attitude that if they do chance on unexpected barriers, they will find resourceful and effective ways to overcome them.

24. Flexibility

Receptive to change, ability to adjust perceptions, goals or action based on an assessment of new information; a rigid, conservative personality is not a trait of a successful entrepreneur.

25. Desire to create

A strong desire to originate an idea or product, to develop something new, to be innovative, to make something happen, to imprint your personality, dreams and ideas on a concept in a unique and different way, requires both the powers of observation and imagination to foresee many possible market ideas.

26. Long-term involvement

Commitment to long-term projects and goals despite considerable personal sacrifice.

27. Self-esteem

Strong sense of self-worth; content to be yourself; good understanding of your strengths and weaknesses; constructively attempt to overcome weak points.

28. Commitment

Dedication to the goal without being distracted or deterred; goal modification may take place, but the ultimate objective is maintained.

29. Innovation

Ability and desire to discover new methods, including new ways of managing the business to be more effective, original ways of marketing the product, or creative ways of improving it. A resourceful approach, constantly improving and changing is characteristic of successful entrepreneurs.

30. Long-term perspective

Comprehension of the long-term goal so that each step of the business plan can be seen in context. This attitude makes the short- and medium-term goals clear and easy to attain. The successful entrepreneur can therefore tolerate substantial frustration and delay by focusing on long-term objectives.

31. Positive outlook

You will need to be an optimist to survive the false starts, near failures, and disappointments that every entrepreneur faces; have to be an objective, pragmatic realist, but must believe that goals can and will be attained.

32. Technical and industrial knowledge

Comprehensive understanding of the industry, and products or service that the business depends on directly; access to resource people with additional knowledge. Anyone who starts a business in an unfamiliar area is risking failure.

33. Human relations

Ability to understand and interact well with people of varying personalities and values. This is important when dealing with employees, bankers, investors, partners, suppliers, or customers and is reflected in characteristics such as sociability, consideration, cheerfulness, cooperation, and tact.

34. Access to financial resources

Ability to obtain funding when needed; awareness of all the funds that might be available and how to obtain them.

35. Desire for money

A respect for money and learning how to deal with it wisely; an ongoing awareness of the factors that influence profit in each part of the business, so that cash flow can be monitored, and prudent decisions made based on risk and profit potential; an understanding of financial and accounting methods.

36. Thinking ability

Includes original, creative, critical, and analytical thinking; an entrepreneur should have an enquiring mind and strive to think effectively. A capacity for problem-solving, especially under pressure, is particularly important.

37. Selling ability

Ability to convince others of the value of the product or service offered; particularly important when talking to bank managers, customers, or sales people or in any form of business negotiation; personal belief in the value of the product or service is a prerequisite.

38. Ability to communicate

Must be able to use words effectively, both orally and in writing, and be able to explain concepts in a way that can be easily understood; ability to present proposals clearly to influence bankers or investors to supply money, to enable employees to understand the exact nature of their job and the results you expect, and to encourage customers to buy.

39. Courage

The will to act on your convictions despite obstacles or personal cost. Successful entrepreneurs frequently give up their jobs to embark on a new venture. Deciding to risk the unknown, at the expense of the security of a regular salary and benefits such as health insurance, pension plans, profit-sharing, and paid holidays, takes a lot of courage. In addition, the prospective entrepreneur frequently has to face friends, family, and spouse who do not always understand or support the desire for self-employment, with all its attendant risk and uncertainty, and the commitment of time, energy, and resources.

40. Age

There is no ideal age for someone starting a business, although having enough life experiences, self-awareness, and self-confidence is important. It is common for people to wait until family and financial demands, or other considerations are reduced. On the other hand, external circumstances such as a lay-off can force a decision earlier than originally planned. Ages 30 to 35 seem to be a time when people consider self-employment. Another significant age bracket is 50 to 55 when your financial situation may have stabilised and children are independent.

41. Family background

Successful entrepreneurs often have a spouse, parent or close relative who operates his or her own business; these individuals can provide networking and financial support, as well as understanding, encouragement, and constructive feedback.

42. Ethnic background

It is fairly common for people who have emigrated to Britain, or who have parents or relatives who have emigrated within one or two generations, to go into their own businesses. There are several theories suggested for this: a history of self-support, desire and capacity to work hard to improve their conditions because of previous hardship, desire to have the best for their children, and access to financial and personal assistance in the business venture from an extended family network.

43. Employment background

Tendency to have experienced difficulty working for others for any length of time because of creative personality, frustration taking directions from others, boredom, or resentment of bureaucratic inflexibility. Other indications of a tendency toward entrepreneurship include history of self-employment at an early age or during late school years: for example, a paper round or a summer painting job, mowing lawns, or gardening.

44. Educational background

Many successful entrepreneurs have not had higher education or even taken O levels. In many cases the school system teaches people to become employees rather than entrepreneurs. The concept of self-employment and being your own boss is normally not presented. However, some colleges have implemented an achievement programme to foster entrepreneurial interest.

Studies reflect that the higher the level of education, the greater the career tracking towards being an employee. There are numerous exceptions, of course. For example, professionals such as lawyers, accountants, doctors, dentists, engineers, and architects are highly educated, yet most end up practising as self-employed small business professionals. In addition, college and university teachers frequently become self-employed independent consultants on a part-time or full-time basis.

You now have a clearer picture of the characteristics of successful entrepreneurs. Compare these with the types of entrepreneur referred to in Chapter 1. The quizzes in Part 2 will provide you with a better understanding of yourself, and which characteristics you have or need to develop.

Part 2
Your Personal Assessment

Personal Entrepreneurial Success Profile Quiz

Section 1

Section 1 of this quiz is designed to determine your entrepreneurial characteristics. Read each question and respond by indicating 'T' for true or 'F' for false. Give your immediate reaction. Be completely honest, so that the quiz will really be useful to you. Complete the quiz in one sitting, and be free from distractions. Approximately 30 minutes should be allowed. After you have completed the quiz, go on to Section 2. *Do not* look at the answer key until you have completed both parts.

T / F

1. When I start a task, I sometimes get so involved I forget what time it is. _____

2. I have a history of different jobs; I tend to be easily bored with routine. _____

3. I have sufficient knowledge in my field and additional courses would not benefit me. _____

4. The feedback I get from staff meetings helps me manage more effectively. _____

5. I rarely have to miss work because of problems with my health. _____

6. I get headaches, stomach aches, or have trouble sleeping when under stress. _____

7. I believe that people become successful primarily through good luck. _____

8. I understand basic bookkeeping and feel comfortable dealing with numbers. _____

T / F

9. I think of a glass of water as being half empty rather than half full. _____

10. When I bought my car or house, I borrowed the money from my own bank because it was convenient. _____

11. When faced with a problem, I always find a new way of overcoming it. _____

12. I worry about what will happen if my plans don't work out. _____

13. When I give directions to others, they generally come back to me for further clarification. _____

14. I feel like I am drifting in life. _____

15. If I do something, and it doesn't work out, I have a tendency to look for fault in others. _____

16. I find it easy to alter my sales technique based on the customer's needs. _____

17. I am usually frustrated with myself when I have played a poor game. _____

18. When a decision has to be made, I can make it easily even though I am not sure of the outcome. _____

19. If I am in a meeting and an impasse develops, I am often able to break the impasse with new points of view. _____

20. When I think of a goal I picture it in my mind. _____

21. I believe a person can start a successful business at any age. _____

22. I believe that educational background makes a difference to success in business. _____

23. After giving a presentation, I like to receive feedback on how I can improve. _____

24. I feel a good sense of equilibrium in my life. _____

25. I generally reject the advice my elders give me. _____

26. When investing my money, I prefer to put it in a long-term deposit rather than risk it on the stock market. _____

27. I don't feel comfortable negotiating a loan with my bank manager. _____

T / F

28. I have taken courses in financial management. _____

29. I get frustrated if I don't receive immediate rewards for my efforts. _____

30. Distractions sometimes cause me to delay my goals. _____

31. I prefer keeping short-term rather than long-term goals. _____

32. I am over 70 years of age. _____

33. When I get involved in something that is important to me, I acquire a missionary zeal. _____

34. I have a strong need for social interaction. _____

35. I believe in the saying, 'The buck stops at the top.' _____

36. Once I make up my mind to do something, I find it difficult or upsetting to change. _____

37. It is easy for me to make small talk. _____

38. People who are highly educated tend to be more successful in business. _____

39. After learning how to do something right the first time, I don't change my approach. _____

40. I get disappointed when things don't go my way. _____

41. I find that I am good at thinking of original ideas. _____

42. I usually feel insecure when someone criticises something I've done. _____

43. My doctor says I should lose some weight. _____

44. My parents were born in the UK. _____

45. I find the administrative side of business confusing. _____

46. I find I can work long hours without getting tired. _____

47. When playing a game of cards, I am a good loser. _____

48. If I run into a stumbling block on a project, I often lose interest in continuing. _____

49. I have a plan of where I want to be financially ten years from now. _____

50. I find it frustrating having to deal with more than one thing at a time. _____

51. I dream about being financially independent. _____

T / F

52. I am between 30 and 55 years of age. _____

53. I did well in my written work at school. _____

54. I don't think others respect me as much as they should. _____

55. If I don't reach my objectives within a short time, I tend to lose interest. _____

56. I find it difficult to perceive a need unless someone points it out. _____

57. I frequently make suggestions on how to improve things on the job. _____

58. If someone disagrees with me, I can always convince them of my point of view. _____

59. I feel good about myself when I get up in the morning. _____

60. My family never talked business at home. _____

61. My family often disagrees with the decisions I make. _____

62. I was born outside the UK. _____

63. When I was young, I had my own paper round. _____

64. In my personal life I have obtained professional advice regarding my career, finances, or marriage. _____

65. I sometimes miss a meal in order to finish what I'm doing. _____

66. I don't allow my work to interfere with my social and recreational life. _____

67. I tend to become involved in other organisations as a volunteer. _____

68. Once I have established a routine, I resist change. _____

69. Others would comment that I use tact and diplomacy when dealing with people. _____

70. When I am at a party, I sometimes eat and drink too much. _____

71. When I am placed in a new situation at work, I quickly sort out what needs to be done. _____

72. I see potential problems as challenges. _____

73. Being independent is more important to me than job security. _____

T / F

74. Sometimes my stubbornness gets in the way of seeing issues clearly. _____

75. I feel ambivalent about giving up my employee benefits and paid holidays for the uncertainty of my own business. _____

76. When I start a weight reduction plan, I continue until I reach my goal. _____

77. When I am pressed for time, I never lose perspective. _____

78. When I come up against unexpected obstacles, I prefer not to continue. _____

79. I enjoy setting long-term goals and then working to attain them. _____

80. I believe in the saying, 'If anything can go wrong, it will'. _____

81. I see creative possibilities in everything I do. _____

82. I get irritated talking to salespeople. _____

83. I feel that through hard work and continued learning I can accomplish my goals. _____

84. I believe in the suggestion box as a technique for obtaining new ideas. _____

85. My father and/or mother have been in business for themselves. _____

86. I subscribe to or read trade magazines in my area of interest. _____

87. Almost all my relatives were born outside the UK. _____

88. I always do what my boss tells me to do, rather than doing it my way. _____

89. Before starting my business I plan to take courses in business management. _____

90. When I meet a business person, I generally ask a lot of questions about his or her line of work. _____

91. I have gone on at least one blind date. _____

92. I usually get called upon to do different things because I am skilled in many areas. _____

93. When given something to do, I prefer to be given a list of specific instructions. _____

T / F

94. I refuse to sign a letter with a typographical error in it. _____

95. Constantly having to deal with problems wears me down. _____

96. I have identified my strengths and weaknesses. _____

97. It doesn't matter whether or not you have O or A levels to be successful in business. _____

98. When I think of starting a business, it scares me to think of the unknown. _____

99. I have a strong desire to improve myself in everything I do. _____

100. I always keep my focus on the 'end of the road'. _____

101. I don't mind admitting my weak points. _____

102. My friends would call me an optimist. _____

103. I avoid making decisions as long as possible because I don't enjoy working out the answers. _____

104. I feel that most of the events in my life are determined by fate. _____

105. After making a decision, I sometimes wonder whether I've made the right one. _____

106. At least one of my grandparents was in business for himself or herself. _____

107. I have been working in my specific field for over five years. _____

108. I can handle a lot of stress without feeling depressed. _____

109. I was born in the UK. _____

110. Bureaucracy doesn't bother me. _____

111. I feel uncomfortable talking with others about the mistakes I have made. _____

112. When I start a task I usually finish it. _____

113. I revise my goals from time to time in the light of changing situations. _____

114. When I am feeling upset, others are usually aware of my problems. _____

115. It is important for me to know that I have a dependable income. _____

T / F

116. I enjoy having authority, but I don't enjoy its responsibility. _____

117. I fantasise about having my own business. _____

118. I have a strong desire to be financially independent for the benefit of my family. _____

119. I would start my own business if I felt right about it, in spite of my family's reservations. _____

120. Once I make up my mind to do something, I do it no matter how difficult. _____

121. When I am dealing with a problem, I tend to get stuck easily. _____

122. Once I set an objective, I don't care how long it takes to attain it. _____

123. I always look at the bright side of life. _____

124. I enjoy selling. _____

125. I brainstorm with my staff or colleagues whenever I need creative ideas. _____

126. I regularly read business magazines. _____

127. Before I make an important decision, I ask for feedback from people I respect. _____

128. I usually take a nap when I get home from work. _____

129. When I feel low it generally takes me a while to get over it. _____

130. When discussing an issue, I try to relate to the other person's situation. _____

131. When working on a project, I take the extra effort to ensure high quality rather than just getting the job done. _____

132. If I were laid off, I know I could find some other source of income. _____

133. If anyone suggests I change my course of action, I resist. _____

134. I thrive on the challenge of solving different problems. _____

135. I don't enjoy being directed by others. _____

136. I tend to make decisions emotionally. _____

T / F

137. People with Master of Business Administration degrees always do well in their own businesses. _____

138. I believe in the saying, 'It's the attitude, not the age, that counts'. _____

139. I don't enjoy speaking to groups of people. _____

140. I take seminars or read books on how to achieve success. _____

141. I get discouraged when I meet impediments to my short-term goals. _____

142. Whenever I need money I always find a way to get it. _____

143. I accept myself the way I am. _____

144. I take courses on how to improve what I do. _____

145. Personal or work pressures make it difficult for me to stick to a goal. _____

146. I am in serious financial difficulty at present. _____

147. I take actions spontaneously rather than plan the process first. _____

148. I have never had experience of supervising people. _____

149. When thinking about money, I believe in the saying, 'Easy come, easy go'. _____

150. I prefer downhill skiing to cross-country skiing. _____

151. Once I've met a challenge I am usually satisfied, and don't need to look for other projects. _____

152. I find I can do many jobs well. _____

153. I consider myself a good listener. _____

154. I have enough money to start my own business. _____

155. I find I have to make things happen. _____

156. If I am faced with a sudden change in plans, I can quickly think of alternatives and decide on a new direction. _____

157. I strongly believe in luck. _____

158. I feel comfortable speaking in front of others. _____

159. I am reluctant to modify my approach once I've make up my mind. _____

T / F

160. No one in my family has ever had his own business. _____

161. My last medical check-up was more than two years ago. _____

162. To increase my expertise in my field of work, I take training courses whenever I can. _____

163. Under pressure, I tend to lose my temper. _____

164. My grandparents were born outside the UK. _____

165. I consider myself smarter than most bosses I have ever had. _____

166. I cheat a little on my income tax. _____

167. I believe in the saying, 'If at first you don't succeed, try, try, try again'. _____

168. If at the end of my working day I have not completed the tasks I have set out to do, I normally put in extra time to complete them. _____

169. I normally start off my day with a list of things to do. _____

170. I don't enjoy working alone. _____

171. I enjoy seeking situations where I can take on extra responsibility. _____

172. I prefer to work with little supervision. _____

173. I find it easy to adapt to different roles within my job. _____

174. I look for new ways of doing things. _____

175. I make friends easily. _____

176. The fear of losing my job causes me great apprehension. _____

177. Before starting a task, I usually assess how much time it should take. _____

178. I am not good at dealing with a multitude of problems at the same time. _____

179. When I set my goals, I don't visualise how it will feel to achieve them. _____

180. I feel I can only maximise my personal development by having control over my career. _____

T / F

181. I have difficulty admitting when I am wrong. ——————

182. I am under 20 years of age. ——————

183. I believe in the saying, 'Nothing ventured, nothing gained'. ——————

184. When I've needed a loan in the past, I've gone to where I could get the best rates. ——————

185. I fully respect myself. ——————

186. Even though reaching a goal seems to take forever, I don't give up easily. ——————

187. I consider myself to be very resourceful in tight situations. ——————

188. It is important that I do something unusual and special with my life. ——————

189. I have never been in debt beyond what I could handle. ——————

190. Normally I research the market and compare prices before I make a large purchase. ——————

191. When I am talking with my spouse, I always try to find a basis for compromise. ——————

192. I believe that I can accomplish anything I set my mind to. ——————

193. I don't feel discouraged when others disagree with my opinions. ——————

194. At least one of my close relatives is self-employed. ——————

195. I follow a regular exercise programme. ——————

196. I have not had any experience in the type of business I am thinking of starting. ——————

197. In a tense situation, I get rattled easily. ——————

198. I have held a position in management. ——————

199. I have discussed my ideas of going into business with others. ——————

200. I keep my evenings and weekends for my personal life and don't let work interfere. ——————

201. I worry when I am in debt. ——————

202. When something doesn't work out, I like to know why. ——————

T / F

203. When I play a sport like golf or tennis I am constantly competing with myself to improve my game. _____

204. I usually have a plan of action before starting a project. _____

205. People consider me a jack-of-all-trades. _____

206. I am always willing to lend a helping hand without being asked. _____

207. When I get involved in a committee or organisation, I seek a leadership role and the responsibility that goes with it. _____

208. I am good at finding creative ways of solving problems. _____

209. The idea of being my own boss appeals to me. _____

210. I find it difficult to see where my business will be five years from now. _____

211. I like to think that what I do helps others. _____

212. I can recognise when I have made a mistake. _____

213. I believe that business training can help me compensate for my lack of higher education. _____

214. I don't feel anxious about giving up my job to start a business. _____

215. I often write letters or memos about business matters. _____

216. I need to keep taking on challenges and testing myself. _____

217. I sometimes lose perspective when my goals aren't met. _____

218. I would have difficulty borrowing money from friends or relatives. _____

219. I need to have the feeling of commitment to a dream. _____

220. At times I don't feel completely comfortable with myself. _____

Section 2

In Chapter 3 you had an opportunity to review the common characteristics of successful entrepreneurs. Now try to rate yourself on these characteristics. Compare yourself with others you know and respect. In the right-hand column, tick the category that is most applicable to your situation. Remember, the purpose is to provide a candid view of yourself, so be as objective and realistic as possible.

After you have completed the quiz, turn to the answer key on page 60 and follow the steps for evaluating your answers. Compare the outcome of your responses in Section 1 with your assessment in Section 2. How consistent were you?

After you have completed your personal self-assessment, ask someone else who knows you well to rate you using Section 2. Colleagues, teachers, professional advisers, relatives, and your spouse may have different views of your past accomplishments and your potential as an entrepreneur. Compare their ratings with your own. Be prepared to alter your ratings after considering their opinions. How accurate a view do you have of yourself?

Remember, no individual can be strong in all categories, and it is not essential for success that you excel at all of them. Anyone who has an unrealistically high rating on most traits could still make unrealistic decisions resulting in business failure. The important point is that you gain a realistic and honest understanding of yourself. You can then improve those areas that showed weakness, or compensate with the expertise of partners or members of your management team.

Entrepreneurial category	Weak		Average		Strong
	1	2	3	4	5
1. Continuous goal-setting					
2. Perseverance					
3. Business knowledge					
4. Dealing with failure					
5. Self-determination					
6. Moderate risk-taking					

	Weak		Average		Strong
	1	2	3	4	5

7. Persistent problem solving

8. Initiative

9. Drive and energy level

10. Willingness to consult experts

11. Physical health

12. Mental and emotional health

13. Tolerance of uncertainty

14. Using feedback

15. Competing against self-imposed standards

16. Seeking personal responsibility

17. Self-confidence

18. Versatility

19. Desire for independence

20. Using positive imagery

21. Sense of purpose

22. Objectivity

23. Achievement-oriented

24. Flexibility

25. Desire to create

26. Long-term involvement

27. Self-esteem

28. Commitment

29. Innovation

30. Long-term perspective

31. Positive outlook

32. Technical and industrial knowledge

33. Human relations

34. Access to financial resources

	Weak		Average		Strong
	1	2	3	4	5

35. Desire for money

36. Thinking ability

37. Selling ability

38. Ability to communicate

39. Courage

(*Note.* The last five characteristics are not included in this rating category: they have been dealt with in Section 1.)

40. Age

41. Family background

42. Ethnic background

43. Employment background

44. Educational background

Answer key

1. Compare your answers to Quiz 1 with the answer key that follows. (The category column refers to one of the 44 common characteristics of entrepreneurs discussed in Chapter 3.) Circle all the answers you got correct.
2. Count the number of circled answers on the answer key. Write the total here:
3. Multiply the above total by 100 and divide by 220. Write that number here: per cent. This gives you the percentage of answers that are correct. The higher the percentage, the greater the possibility that you are suited to be an entrepreneur, and the closer you are to exhibiting the characteristics of successful entrepreneurs. If you received less than 60 per cent on the quiz, you should seriously reconsider whether or not you are suited to being in your own business. Complete the rest of the book and honestly assess your potential for success.
4. Now look at the summary of question numbers under each category (page 64). There were five questions asked in each category. This will tell you what questions were considered to fall under specific entrepreneurial characteristic categories. Circle your correct answers on the summary

sheet from the answer key. Count the total correct answers and place that number beside each category. For example, if you answered questions 49, 151 and 169 correctly, you would circle those numbers under 'continuous goal setting' and score 3 out of 5 for that category.

5. Compare your individual category totals above with your self-assessment ratings under each category in Quiz 2.

You should now have a better understanding of your areas of specific strength and weakness. This will assist you to deal with the weak areas more effectively.

Question	Answer	Category	Question	Answer	Category
1.	T	9	30.	F	28
2.	T	43	31.	F	30
3.	F	32	32.	F	40
4.	T	14	33.	T	21
5.	T	11	34.	F	19
6.	F	11	35.	T	16
7.	F	5	36..	F	24
8.	T	35	37.	T	33
9.	F	31	38.	F	44
10.	F	34	39.	F	29
11.	T	29	40.	T	31
12.	F	23	41.	T	25
13.	F	38	42.	F	17
14.	F	21	43.	F	11
15.	F	16	44.	F	42
16.	T	24	45.	F	3
17.	T	15	46.	T	9
18.	T	13	47.	F	4
19.	T	8	48.	F	2
20.	T	20	49.	T	1
21.	T	40	50.	F	18
22.	F	44	51.	T	20
23.	T	14	52.	T	40
24.	T	12	53.	T	38
25.	F	10	54.	F	27
26.	F	6	55.	F	26
27.	F	37	56.	F	25
28.	T	35	57.	T	36
29.	F	26	58.	T	37

Question	Answer	Category	Question	Answer	Category
59.	T	17	101.	T	27
60.	F	41	102.	T	31
61.	F	12	103.	F	36
62.	T	42	104.	F	5
63.	T	43	105.	F	17
64.	T	10	106.	T	41
65.	T	9	107.	T	32
66.	F	2	108.	T	12
67.	T	8	109.	F	42
68.	F	24	110.	F	43
69.	T	33	111.	F	4
70.	F	15	112.	T	2
71.	T	13	113.	T	1
72.	T	7	114.	F	33
73.	T	19	115.	F	13
74.	F	22	116.	F	16
75.	F	39	117.	T	20
76.	T	28	118.	T	21
77.	T	30	119.	T	39
78.	F	23	120.	T	28
79.	T	26	121.	F	29
80.	F	31	122.	T	26
81.	T	25	123.	T	31
82.	F	37	124.	T	37
83.	T	5	125.	T	14
84.	T	14	126.	T	3
85.	T	41	127.	T	10
86.	T	32	128.	F	9
87.	T	42	129.	F	4
88.	F	43	130.	T	33
89.	T	3	131.	T	15
90.	T	10	132.	T	13
91.	T	6	133.	F	24
92.	T	18	134.	T	7
93.	F	8	135.	T	19
94.	T	15	136.	F	22
95.	F	7	137.	F	44
96.	T	22	138.	T	40
97.	T	44	139.	F	38
98.	F	39	140.	T	23
99.	T	23	141.	F	30
100.	T	30	142.	T	34

Question	Answer	Category	Question	Answer	Category
143.	T	27	182.	F	40
144.	T	29	183.	T	39
145.	F	28	184.	T	34
146.	F	35	185.	T	27
147.	F	36	186.	T	26
148.	F	3	187.	T	29
149.	F	35	188.	T	25
150.	T	6	189.	F	35
151.	F	1	190.	T	36
152.	T	18	191.	T	37
153.	T	38	192.	T	5
154.	T	34	193.	T	17
155.	T	25	194.	T	41
156.	T	36	195.	T	11
157.	F	5	196.	F	32
158.	T	17	197.	F	12
159.	F	14	198.	T	3
160.	F	41	199.	T	10
161.	F	11	200.	F	9
162.	T	32	201.	F	6
163.	F	12	202.	T	4
164.	T	42	203.	T	2
165.	T	43	204.	T	1
166.	T	6	205.	T	18
167.	T	4	206.	T	8
168.	T	2	207.	T	16
169.	T	1	208.	T	7
170.	F	19	209.	T	19
171.	T	16	210.	F	20
172.	T	8	211.	T	21
173.	T	18	212.	T	22
174.	T	24	213.	T	44
175.	T	33	214.	T	39
176.	F	13	215.	T	38
177.	T	15	216.	T	23
178.	F	7	217.	F	30
179.	F	20	218.	F	34
180.	T	21	219.	T	28
181.	F	22	220.	F	27

Summary of question numbers under each category

Category	Question number
1. Continuous goal-setting	49, 113, 151, 169, 204
2. Perseverance	48, 66, 112, 168, 203
3. Business knowledge	45, 89, 126, 148, 198
4. Dealing with failure	47, 111, 129, 167, 202
5. Self-determination	7, 83, 104, 157, 192
6. Moderate risk-taking	26, 91, 150, 166, 201
7. Persistent problem-solving	72, 95, 134, 178, 208
8. Initiative	19, 67, 93, 172, 206
9. Drive and energy level	1, 46, 65, 128, 200
10. Willingness to consult experts	25, 64, 90, 127, 199
11. Physical health	5, 6, 43, 161, 195
12. Mental and emotional health	24, 61, 108, 163, 197
13. Tolerance of uncertainty	18, 71, 115, 132, 176
14. Using feedback	4, 23, 84, 125, 159
15. Competing against self-imposed standards	17, 70, 94, 131, 177
16. Seeking personal responsibility	15, 35, 116, 171, 207
17. Self-confidence	42, 59, 105, 158, 193
18. Versatility	50, 92, 152, 173, 205
19. Desire for independence	34, 135, 170, 209, 220
20. Using positive imagery	20, 51, 117, 179, 210
21. Sense of purpose	14, 33, 118, 180, 211
22. Objectivity	74, 96, 136, 181, 212
23. Achievement-oriented	12, 78, 99, 140, 216
24. Flexibility	16, 36, 68, 133, 174
25. Desire to create	41, 56, 81, 155, 188
26. Long-term involvement	29, 55, 79, 122, 186
27. Self-esteem	54, 101, 143, 185, 220
28. Commitment	20, 76, 120, 145, 219
29. Innovation	11, 39, 121, 144, 187
30. Long-term perspective	31, 77, 100, 141, 217

Category	Question number
31. Positive outlook	9, 40, 80, 102, 123
32. Technical and industrial knowledge	3, 86, 107, 162, 196
33. Human relations	37, 69, 114, 130, 175
34. Access to financial resources	10, 142, 154, 184, 218
35. Desire for money	8, 28, 146, 149, 189
36. Thinking ability	57, 103, 147, 156, 190
37. Selling ability	27, 58, 82, 124, 191
38. Ability to communicate	13, 53, 139, 153, 215
39. Courage	75, 98, 119, 183, 214
40. Age	21, 32, 52, 138, 182
41. Family background	60, 85, 106, 160, 194
42. Ethnic background	44, 62, 87, 109, 164
43. Employment background	2, 63, 88, 110, 165
44. Educational background	22, 38, 97, 137, 213

Quiz 2

Ranking Your Entrepreneurial Traits Quiz

Questions

No single entrepreneur possesses all of the traits or characteristics described in Chapter 3, nor are all those characteristics needed to be successful. But which of the traits and characteristics are most commonly shared and most important for success?

In order to assess what you believe to be important entrepreneurial abilities, complete the following quiz. Rate the quality on a scale of 1 to 5. A rating of 1 indicates little importance, and a rating of 5 indicates great importance.

Characteristics	Little importance			Great importance	
	1	2	3	4	5
1. A strong need to achieve					
2. A need to associate closely with others					
3. An ability to get along with employees					
4. A willingness to tolerate uncertainty					
5. Good physical health					
6. A high level of energy					
7. A willingness to take risks					
8. Self-confidence					
9. Innovation					
10. Ability to lead effectively					

	Little importance			Great importance	
	1	2	3	4	5

11. Patience

12. A strong desire for money

13. Being well organised

14. A desire to create

15. A need for power

16. Perseverance

17. Self-reliance

18. Desire and willingness to take the initiative

19. Competitiveness

20. Versatility

Now that you have rated the various entrepreneurial characteristics, rank the characteristics in order of importance in your opinion under one of the following three categories:

(a) Most important for success
   (include those characteristics that you numbered 4 and 5)
(b) Important for success
   (include those characteristics that you gave a rating of 3)
(c) Least important for success
   (include those characteristics that you rated numbers 1 and 2)

Most important	Important	Least important
_____	_____	_____
_____	_____	_____
_____	_____	_____
_____	_____	_____
_____	_____	_____
_____	_____	_____
_____	_____	_____

After you have completed your ranking, turn to the answer key. These responses came from studies of a large number of successful entrepreneurs who were asked to indicate what personal characteristics they felt were most important to entrepreneurial success. How did your ranking compare?

Answer key

Studies have shown that entrepreneurs rate these abilities or qualities in the following order of importance:

Most important for success

Perseverance
Desire and willingness to take the initiative
Competitiveness
Self-reliance
A strong need to achieve
Self-confidence
Good physical health.

Important for success

A willingness to take risks
A high level of energy
An ability to get along with employees
Versatility
A desire to create
Innovation.

Least important for success

Ability to lead effectively
A willingness to tolerate uncertainty
A strong desire for money
Patience
Being well organised
A need for power
A need to closely associate with others.

Quiz 3

Management Skills Evaluation Quiz

Now that you have assessed your entrepreneurial traits, you still have to evaluate your management skills. If you lack some of the skills needed in your business venture, they can be provided by partners or others on your management team, but only if you perceive the need for such skills and are aware of your personal shortcomings.

It is very important to examine your managerial experience and accomplishments in various key roles realistically. The following quiz breaks down these roles into their principal functions. Rate yourself on each one. Remember that the functions critical to your success as an entrepreneur may vary depending upon the type of business venture and the structure of your business.

You will rate yourself on a six-point scale from no skill to strong skills. Mark the column that you feel most accurately represents your skill at this time. Here is an explanation of each category:

A *None.* No known skill

B *Weak.* Unfamiliar with skill area or poor knowledge; may need someone else on a full-time basis

C *Below average.* Between average and weak

D *Average.* Have limited knowledge and may require assistance from time to time

E *Above average.* Between strong and average

F *Strong.* Know thoroughly and have proven ability

69

General management and administration

A B C D E F

1. Problem solving

(a) Ability to anticipate potential problems and avoid them

(b) Ability to analyse and plan effective action to resolve problems

(c) Ability to deal with the details of particular problems

(d) Ability to resolve problems quickly

2. Planning

(a) Ability to set realistic and attainable goals

(b) Ability to identify obstacles to achieving the goals

(c) Ability to develop strategic plans for overcoming obstacles

(d) Ability to develop detailed action plans to achieve the goals

(e) Ability to plan own time effectively

3. Decision making

(a) Ability to make decisions quickly and easily

(b) Ability to make decisions on your best analysis of incomplete data

(c) Ability to make decisions free from doubt

4. Project management

(a) Skill in organising project teams

(b) Skill in setting project goals

(c) Skill in defining project tasks

(d) Skill in monitoring task completion

(d) Skill in dealing with project

(e) problems

5. Communication

(a) Ability to communicate clearly in

A B C D E F

writing to the public, customers,
colleagues and subordinates
   (b) Ability to communicate clearly
   with the public, customers,
   colleagues and subordinates verbally
   (c) Knowledge of effective public
   speaking techniques
   (d) Ability as a public speaker

6. Personnel administration

   (a) Ability to set up payroll system
   (b) Ability to recruit personnel
   (c) Ability to train personnel
   (d) Ability to dismiss personnel

7. Negotiating

   (a) Ability to negotiate effectively
   (b) Ability to balance quickly the
   value given and value received
   (c) Knowledge of negotiating skills
   and techniques

8. Time management

   (a) Knowledge of the skills necessary
   for effective time management
   (b) Effective application of time
   management skills

9. Stress management

   (a) Knowledge of skills necessary for
   effective stress management
   (b) Effective application of stress
   management skills

10. Overall administrative skills

Give yourself an overall rating reflecting
your level of skill in all aspects of
administrative management

71

A B C D E F

Operations management

1. Manufacturing management

    (a) Knowledge of the production processes, manpower, space and equipment required to produce your product

    (b) Experience managing production of products within established criteria

2. Stock control

    (a) Familiarity with techniques for controlling materials inventories

3. Quality control

    (a) Ability to set up inspection systems and standards for quality control at all stages of production

4. Purchasing

    (a) Ability to identify the best sources of supply

    (b) Familiarity with techniques for purchasing at the best price

    (c) Ability to negotiate contracts with suppliers

    (d) Ability to manage flow of incoming product into stock

5. Overall operations skills

Give yourself an overall rating reflecting your level of skill in all aspects of operations management

Research, development and engineering

1. Direction and management of applied research

    (a) Ability to distinguish and keep a

A B C D E F

cautious balance between long-range projects and shorter-range research

2. Management of development

(a) Ability to plan and direct the work of development engineers so that production engineering needs can be met

3. Technical knowledge

(a) Ability to contribute personally to research, development and/or engineering

4. Management of engineering

(a) Ability to plan and direct engineers in the design and testing of the manufacture of the new product

5. Overall research, development, and engineering skills

Give yourself an overall rating reflecting your level of skill in all aspects of research, development, and engineering

Financial management

1. Raising capital

(a) Ability to decide how best to acquire funds
(b) Ability to forecast the need for funds and to prepare budgets
(c) Familiarity with sources and means of short- and long-term financing
(d) Experience negotiating with lenders
(e) Experience negotiating with investors

A B C D E F

2. Money management

(a) Familiarity with bookkeeping, accounting, and control systems

(b) Ability to design, install, maintain, and use financial controls

(c) Ability to set up a project cost control system, analyse overheads, prepare profit and loss accounts, and balance sheets

(d) Experience dealing with government regulations

(e) Ability to manage a bookkeeper

3. Specific financial skills

(a) Ability to prepare a cash flow analysis

(b) Ability to prepare a break-even analysis

(c) Knowledge of budgeting and profit planning techniques

(d) Understanding of profit and loss accounts

(e) Understanding of balance sheet

4. Credit and collection management

(a) Ability to develop credit policies and approval criteria

(b) Understanding procedures for ageing debtors and creditors

(c) Understanding various collection techniques

(d) Understanding when to commence legal action

5. Overall financial skills

Give yourself an overall rating reflecting your level of skill in all aspects of financial management

A B C D E F

Personnel Management

1. Leadership

  (a) Understanding the concepts of leadership

  (b) Understanding the techniques of leadership

  (c) Ability to lead when necessary

  (d) Ability to supervise and control activities of others effectively

2. Listening

  (a) Effective listening skills to hear what the person is really saying

  (b) Understanding non-verbal messages

3. Criticism

  (a) Ability to provide performance and interpersonal criticism to others in a non-threatening manner, so that the effect is practical and well received

  (b) Ability to receive feedback from others without becoming defensive or argumentative and to use feedback constructively

4. Helping

  (a) Ability to determine when assistance is needed

  (b) Ability to ask for assistance

  (c) Ability to provide assistance

5. Teamwork

Ability to work effectively with others to pursue common goals

6. Conflict resolution

  (a) Ability to deal with differences directly

75

A B C D E F

(b) Ability to resolve differences quickly
and amicably

7. Selecting and developing subordinates

(a) Ability to select subordinates
(b) Ability to delegate responsibility
to subordinates
(c) Ability to assist subordinates to
develop their managerial capabilities
(d) Ability to assess the performance
of subordinates

8. Climate building

(a) Ability to create a work atmosphere
conducive to high performance
(b) Knowledge of techniques for
rewarding high performance

9. Overall interpersonal skills

Give yourself an overall rating reflecting
your level of skill in all aspects of
personnel management

Marketing and sales

1. Market research and evaluation

(a) Familiarity with questionnaire
design and sampling techniques
(b) Ability to design and conduct
market research studies
(c) Ability to interpret the results
of research

2. Strategic sales

(a) Experience developing marketing
strategies
(b) Experience planning suitable
advertising and promotion
programmes

A B C D E F

(c) Experience setting up an effective distribution or sales representative network

3. Sales management and merchandising

(a) Ability to analyse sales potential of different territories
(b) Ability to manage sales force to obtain a target share of market
(c) Ability to provide merchandising support to a direct sales force

4. Direct selling

(a) Experience identifying potential customers
(b) Experience using direct sales techniques
(c) Experience successfully closing sales

5. Service

(a) Ability to perceive service a product needs
(b) Experience handling customer complaints
(c) Experience managing a service organisation

6. Distribution management

(a) Familiarity with despatch costs, scheduling procedures and carriers
(b) Ability to organise and manage the flow of the product to the customer

7. Overall marketing skills

Give yourself an overall rating reflecting your level of skill in all aspects of marketing and sales

77

A B C D E F

Legal and tax aspects

1. Company law

(a) Familiarity with the legal differences between incorporation, partnership, and sole trader

(b) Familiarity with the services to look for when selecting a solicitor

(c) Familiarity with types of security documentation requested by banks and the effect of pledging that security

(d) Familiarity with the negative aspects of signing a personal guarantee to a bank, trade creditor, or leasing company

(e) Familiarity with the process of litigation

2. Contract law

(a) Familiarity with types of leases and their financial implications

(b) Familiarity with the advantages of having a contract in writing rather than a verbal one

(c) Familiarity with the legal aspects and benefits of a shareholder's agreement

(d) Familiarity with the legal aspects and benefits of a management contract

(e) Familiarity with the legal aspects and benefits of a buy-sell agreement

(f) Familiarity with government contract procedures and requirements, if you are intending to sell goods or services to government departments

3. Patent law

(a) Knowledge of when to patent, register a trade mark, design, or copyright

(b) General knowledge of the procedures

A B C D E F

to register patent, trade mark, design, and copyright

(c) Familiarity with services to look for when selecting a patent agent

4. Tax law

(a) Familiarity with allowable expenses and deductible expenses

(b) Familiarity with the services to look for when selecting a qualified tax accountant

(c) Familiarity with reporting requirements for business

(d) Familiarity with tax advantages of fringe benefits and so on

5. Overall legal and tax skills

Give yourself an overall rating reflecting your level of skill in all aspects of the law and taxation

Now that you have completed the Management Skills Quiz, you should have a very good understanding of your strengths and weaknesses. Individuals are rarely equally strong in all the functions of any role. You should realise that it could be risky to generalise about your ability to perform an entire role because of strength in one or two of its functions.

List and rank your five strongest management skills and your five weakest management skills:

Strongest management skills

_____

_____

_____

_____

_____

Weakest management skills

_____

_____

_____

_____

The next step is to review the evaluation of your management skills with people who know you best on a day-to-day basis; for example, past or present co-workers. Your colleagues, subordinates, and bosses may see different aspects of your abilities at each skill.

Write down all the skills that scored A, B, C or D after you received the input of others. If those areas are important to your business success, detail your plan for improving your skill in those areas, or for otherwise compensating for them.

You have now developed what should be an accurate assessment of your management skills. You should be in a much better position to evaluate realistically the personal risk that you will be faced with if you decide to start and manage your own business.

Part 3
Setting Up

Chapter 4

Searching for Business Opportunities

There are unlimited business opportunities if you know how and where to find them. But having found them, most people do not know how to choose the best. In this chapter you will learn the sources of business opportunities and the techniques for an effective search.

Sources of ideas and opportunities

1. Yellow Pages

The Yellow Pages lists every product or service relating to small business. Turn to the cross-referenced index at the front and methodically work your way through the listings. Look for the types of business that supply products or services in an area that interests you. For example, if you are interested in gardening, you would look up all the cross-referenced classifications associated with gardening. That would include florists, nurseries and landscape architects.

2. Public library

Your public library is an invaluable source of business ideas, opportunities and information. The reference librarian will help you gain access to an extensive range of information relevant to your business interests. Look for the business and economics, science and technology, and financial management departments. The library is full of business-related books, directories, trade publications, and newspapers.

3. Business transfer agents

These people buy or sell businesses on behalf of clients.

Their role is to do a detailed analysis and assessment of the business for the purpose of purchase or sale.

4. Estate agents

Many estate agents also buy and sell businesses. You could contact some of the top-selling ones, advise them of the types of business you are interested in, and ask them to notify you if any become available.

5. Accountants, solicitors, and consultants

Professional accountants in private practice frequently deal with a variety of clients. They are aware of each business's current financial situation and past history, as well as its future plans. If you have an accountant, ask him or her if he/she knows of any potential business opportunities in your area of interest. They may know of a client whose business is for sale, or a client who needs equity participation or management expertise. They may have clients who have good ideas but are looking for a partner to make the idea a reality, or they may have clients looking for investments.

Like accountants, solicitors also deal with business clients, especially those solicitors who practise commercial law. If you have your own solicitor, or have a friend who is a solicitor, express your interest in looking for specific business opportunities.

Consultants and professional advisers can help you with a specific problem. They can give specific feedback, provide new ideas, and help you plan your business venture.

6. Business administration courses

The faculty of business administration at colleges and universities have business skills in diverse areas. You may want to find out who the faculty are and their areas of expertise. They could be possible venture partners or investors, or you could engage them as consultants. You may want graduate students to do research for you.

7. Acting as a self-employed consultant

If you are a consultant in a technical area, you could obtain venture ideas by consulting other entrepreneurs who need your specialised service. You could target inventors or researchers who could be potential sources of new product ideas. Out of this relationship could develop a partnership or joint venture arrangement to develop or market a product.

8. Newspapers and magazines

Subscribe to your local daily newspaper for business ideas and look in *The Times*, *Guardian*, *Daily Telegraph*, *Financial Times*, *Observer*, *Sunday Times* and *Sunday Telegraph*. Your public library will carry these and other newspapers.

Business magazines also have classified ads that may provide some ideas, such as *Your Business*, *British Business* (Department of Trade and Industry), *The Economist* and regional business journals. A list can be extracted from a study of *British Rate and Data*, which should be in most good reference libraries.

You may wish to place an ad yourself, seeking responses by interested parties to your business ideas or investment opportunities. You may want to advertise for a specific type of business.

Newspaper and magazine articles are also a rich source of material and full of money-making ideas. As you read an article, think of the business opportunities that might exist, or the trends that might develop.

9. Business subscriber publications

Venture Capital Report is a monthly publication. Each edition profiles around 10 businesses seeking investment and, sometimes, management input too. Available from VCR, 20 Baldwin Street, Bristol BS1 1SE, or on view at the Science Reference Library in London. Annual subscription £180. *Business Link-up* contains advertisements for investors and/or partners. It is published monthly from 33 George Street, London W1R 9FA. Annual subscription £60.

10. Books

Many business books are available in specialist bookshops that are not in public libraries. Libraries have limited budgets, or may concentrate on other subject areas. You can look at a publication at your main library called *Books in Print*, which lists all available titles by subject heading. It is up-dated annually. Most bookshops will order a book for you on request.

11. Foreign publications

The commercial departments of foreign consulates may be helpful; also large city business libraries, and the Science Reference Library in London.

12. Trade publications

Subscribe to trade publications in your field of interest, or read them at your public library. A list of trade publications can be obtained from the resource books, *British Rate and Data* or *Benn's Media Directory*, found in most libraries. Trade journals are usually the first to publicise a new product. In many cases the manufacturer is looking for help in distri-buting a new line. The ads will also provide information about your competitors and their products. They are some of the best sources of data about a specific industry, and fre-quently print market surveys, forecasts, and articles on needs the industry may have. All this information provides a stimulating source of ideas.

13. Government agencies

The Small Firms Service of the Department of Employment was set up to assist the entrepreneur with advice, business management courses, publications, and other help. You can also obtain feedback on the viability of your business idea. The initial consultation is free. The counsellors are generally experts who have practical experience in business.

The Council for Small Industries in Rural Areas provides an advice and training service for small firms in English towns and villages with under 10,000 population. It can also help with finance in certain circumstances.

In Scotland and Wales a similar service is offered by the Scottish Development Agency and the Welsh Development Agency respectively.

Throughout the United Kingdom there are local develop-ment agencies which will be found in the telephone book;

they offer advice and help to small businesses and are likely to be very knowledgeable about local schemes which can provide financial assistance and workshop space.

Your public library can provide you with further information on all the government departments relevant to your area of interest, and how to get on free mailing lists, or government source lists for the goods or services that you may want to provide.

14. Venture capital companies

Venture capital companies provide investment for businesses, often in exchange for a share in the equity. Investment can be made through the Business Expansion Scheme which offers tax relief on investments left in approved funds for five years. They continually examine existing and potential businesses. If you contact these companies and let them know of your interest, you could have the opportunity to invest in a business or product.

15. Friends and acquaintances

Friends are always a source of ideas. Advise them of your interest in looking for specific products or services. When you are at a social function, ask people what they do. If they are in business, ask them questions about the business, such as why they got started, what their future plans are, where they see a need in the market, and what they enjoy about their business. You could pick up many ideas, as well as possible opportunities. Think of all the people you know socially. If any of them work in your area of interest, take them to lunch and ask them about their businesses. Tell them you are exploring the possibility of going into your own business.

16. Competitors

Determine who your competitors are and then closely examine their products or services. Determine if the product or service could be improved.

17. Potential customers

Customers can be an excellent source of information about

market needs and where an existing product or service is inadequate. You should be clear enough about the product you want to make, or the service you want to provide, to identify potential customers. You could then meet them to discuss your plans, as part of your research.

18. Distributors and wholesalers

If you are interested in selling or manufacturing a product, contact those people who distribute the kinds of product you are interested in. Distributors and wholesalers have an extensive knowledge of the strong and weak points of existing products. They should also know the type of product improvements and new products that are needed by their customers.

19. Former employers

You should reflect on your current and prior employment, and determine whether anything you have done or are doing suggests a product or service idea that could be the basis of a business venture. You may be interested in a product or service that is similar or related to a product or service provided by a former employer. It would be prudent to seek the advice of a solicitor before you embark on your plans, to satisfy yourself that your idea does not infringe on a prior employer's trade secrets, patents, or other proprietary knowledge. You will want to ensure that you don't have an employment contract restricting you from competing with your former employer for a fixed period of time after your departure.

20. Hobbies and travel

Think of the areas relating to your hobby or leisure activities where you believe a need exists. For example, packaging your skill and knowledge by writing a book, pamphlet, or newsletter could be successful.

Whenever you travel, look for new business opportunities. Many products and services may not have been introduced into the United Kingdom. You may be able to negotiate exclusive or distribution rights for a product. You may want to duplicate the product or service yourself, as long as it does not infringe any legal rights that the owner might have.

21. Franchising and licensing

If you are already in business, you might want to franchise or license your idea. A franchise means that another person can use your business concept for a fee but must operate within the guidelines that you establish. There are various types of franchise arrangements, discussed in the next chapter.

Licensing means renting the right to manufacture or distribute a product within agreed stipulations. The owner of the licence retains ownership, then receives a royalty or fixed fee from the licensee. You may want to contact a licence broker or patent agent about the right to manufacture or provide a service. Licence brokers represent companies searching for licensees and companies seeking a product to license.

22. Exporting and importing

As mentioned in earlier examples, there are numerous opportunities for export to other countries. Once you have identified the need that your product meets, it is then a matter of using your ingenuity to find distributors who will test your product in a foreign market to determine if the same need exists there. Contact the British Overseas Trade Board. The offices are listed in the phone book. You can obtain free assistance through them.

23. Partnership with inventor

You may wish to find an inventor with a product to sell. There are various contacts referred to in this chapter, including patent agents and brokers.

24. Patents

Patent brokers act as agents for individuals or organisations seeking to sell an invention or patent. They specialise in marketing patents owned by individual inventors, corporations, universities, or other research organisations, to entrepreneurs seeking products that will be commercially viable. Some brokers also specialise in international product licensing.

Patent agents specialise in all aspects of patent and related areas of law. They act for clients selling patents or inventions, and those wanting to buy them.

25. Product licensing information services

An excellent way to obtain information about the large number of product ideas available from independent inventors, corporations, or universities is to subscribe to a service that periodically publishes data on products offered for licensing, such as *International Licensing* (92 Cannon Lane, Pinner, Middlesex) or *Technology Transfer International* (15 Selvage Lane, Mill Hill, London NW7 3SS).

26. Seminars

There are many seminars, workshops and courses available on both small business management and entrepreneurship. They are taught by private companies, or by government agencies, colleges and universities, and trade and management associations. Seminars offer an excellent opportunity to meet large numbers of people with interests similar to yours. You should make a determined effort to talk with other business people attending the seminar during the interval.

27. Trade and business associations

Stimulating ideas can be developed by belonging to a trade association in your area of interest. Frequently they will maintain a library of material that is available to members. There are also meetings, newsletters, and magazines. Attending trade association meetings and talking to the sales representatives there can be a good way of assessing the competition. Business associations include chambers of commerce, Lions, Rotarians, and many other groups. These associations provide an ideal opportunity to network with business people.

For further information, look in the Yellow Pages under 'associations'. They are all listed in *Directory of British Associations* (CBD Research) which should be in your local reference library.

28. Examine existing products

There are many products in great demand, but few people know about them because of ineffective marketing. Investigate products that you think have a possibility of success.

Find out the marketing methods that were used. You might pick up that product's distribution rights at a low price.

If the product was previously popular and has a nostalgic value, you may wish to repackage it and target the same market as before. If the product is novel or decorative, you might find a new market with each new generation.

There are also many innovative ways of modifying or repackaging an existing product to appeal to new markets. For example, there could be a consumer version of an industrial product. There could be foreign market possibilities that have never been explored.

Sometimes products are made using obsolete, expensive, complicated, or heavy material. With some research you may find new material that would be state of the art, inexpensive, simple and lightweight. Look for modifications that will improve the marketability and profit of the product.

You might also look for products or services that complement each other to gain greater profit. For example, a grocery retail outlet could sublet space to a video rental outlet. The traffic for one store would benefit the other.

29. Capitalise on trends

Try to pinpoint trends in the early stages so that you can benefit as the trend grows. For example, many fitness clubs started because of a trend towards physical fitness and good health. If you saw this trend developing because you read sport publications and newspaper articles, you could have started a fitness club, and multiplied its services throughout the city or in adjacent towns. You could have done so inexpensively by renting church halls and getting free media publicity. When the trend started to peak you would have consolidated your presence in the market, making it easier to fend off latecomer operations. Of course, with any trend you must also watch for the downslide. Get out before the trend fizzles, and try to sell at a high market price.

30. Changing government policy and regulations

Whenever a new government assumes power, there is change in policies and regulations. Whenever change occurs, opportunities exist to market your product or service. For example, if the government has a policy of deregulation, then every business that was previously protected by regulation will now face increased competition. Their business survival could be at stake. An enterprising consultant with expertise in the affected area could take advantage of the opportunity created by the change. He or she could target potential clients and offer an advisory service to help the business survive and succeed. A successful consultant is always looking for potential clients by thinking of ways to help a client to save more money, make more money, or help the client operate more effectively.

Another policy change now in operation is to privatise government services whenever possible. The purpose of this policy is to save money by cutting existing staff levels. Government services are then contracted out to the private sector whenever possible.

31. Economic changes

Whenever the economy changes, new problems, challenges, and opportunities arise. For example, when the economy is bad there could be an increased market for a second-hand clothes shop. When the economy is buoyant, there would be an increased demand for businesses in the leisure and travel business. A solicitor who deals mainly in conveyancing and business law makes fees on conveyancing and mortgages, and on the increase in incorporations and the processing of bank security documentation. When the economy is poor, fees are made on foreclosures and litigation, including collection work.

Creative ways of looking at ideas

Now that you have started thinking of ideas, look at each concept from many different points of view. Here is a list of variables to consider when thinking about a product or service. This list does not include every approach, and you will certainly think of additional questions. Write them down so you can refer back to them. Ask yourself the following questions:

How can I . . .

- make it safer, cleaner, slower, or faster?

- make it at home and save overheads?
- contract out to other people who make the product or perform the service at their home?
- teach it more quickly?
- make it more convenient or inexpensive?
- make it more pleasant?
- cut costs of material and labour?
- combine it with or add it on to other products or services?
- make it automatic?
- make it easier to package, store, transport?
- make it self-contained, portable, mobile, or disposable?
- condense or enlarge its size?
- make it easier to use?
- make it less expensive to replace, repair or re-use?
- make it easier to clean, maintain, lubricate, or adjust?
- make it more attractive and appealing?
- make it lighter, stronger, adjustable, thinner, or foldable?
- make it quieter or louder?
- minimise its potential hazards?
- exert less effort, time, and energy when dealing with it?
- add new features?
- accessorise it?
- make it reversible?
- make it dual or multi-functional?
- sell it more cheaply for more benefit (eg two for the price of one)?
- remove any irritating features or side effects?
- improve its availability or distribution?
- improve its production?
- improve its design?
- improve its marketing?
- improve it in other ways?

Techniques for generating ideas

Don't limit your search to one idea at a time; develop nine or ten until one clearly emerges as the strongest. You are constantly reviewing random input from information you read, see, or hear. Considering a number of interesting ideas will make it more likely that you'll find uses for the information you absorb. If you limit yourself to a single idea at an early stage in your search, you could convince yourself that you are committed to that idea before you are really ready.

How do you train your mind to discover and create new business opportunities? The following techniques will effectively generate new ideas. Not all these techniques will work for everyone. Try them all and see which work for you. Remember to keep notes on your ideas in a binder for easy reference.

1. Brainstorming

The basic steps in brainstorming are simple:

(a) Organise a group of friends, colleagues, or relatives with very different backgrounds, experiences, and skills. The purpose is to derive new business ideas and inventions from combining known ideas and mechanisms in new ways. When you bring diverse personalities together you will enhance the possibility of unusual and creative ideas being developed.

(b) Prepare the group for the meeting. Inform the participants of the problems to be discussed a few days in advance. This allows the unconscious mind to start to find creative solutions.

(c) Don't evaluate ideas as good or bad during the first phase. You and your group are simply generating ideas. It is important to appreciate the difference between idea creation and idea screening. Encourage everyone to express all ideas freely.

(d) Emphasise volume, not quality, in idea generation. Encourage everyone to generate as many ideas as possible in a short period of time. Accept foolish, silly, mediocre, and good ideas. Request that each participant think of 25 business ideas in 10 minutes and write them down. Remember, don't be critical of the quality of ideas. It will stifle the creativity. Studies show that only by expressing many ideas do you end up with a few good ones. Note them all.

(e) Build on each other's ideas; benefit from the diverse group with different backgrounds, personalities, and experiences. Don't pass judgement.

(f) Sort out the ideas after the meeting is over. Analyse your selection of ideas by reflecting on them, grouping them together, expanding them and then choosing what you consider to be the best.

These principles can be applied to your own idea search if you can't get a group together. Think of as many business ideas as possible on your own. Include ideas that you have thought of in the past, or those you have heard about. Write them all down in random order. Don't try to evaluate them or worry about how feasible they might be. Later, you can go through the same organisation process discussed above.

2. Imagery

This concept was mentioned in Chapter 3 in the discussion of characteristics of entrepreneurs. This is a means of turning your dream into reality. Focus on the dream, and then the unconscious will assist in the realisation of that vision. The unconscious mind will continue to monitor and adjust the goals to maintain the objective. During the imagery process new ideas are considered, assessed and rejected, or accepted.

3. Cross-fertilisation

The cross-fertilisation concept involves searching out individuals who have different disciplines, ideas, and experiences, and setting up brainstorming opportunities. This is generally done on a one-to-one basis, perhaps over lunch or dinner. It can be stultifying to interact only with people of like mind, occupation, roles, experiences, and background. If you want more ideas, seek out more sources of stimulation and let your mind run free.

4. Curiosity

When you are curious about something, act on your curiosity

and check it out. Ideas without action are soon forgotten and lost, but people who pay attention to their ideas can follow leads playfully and keep them alive and moving forward. When you have ideas, get into the habit of making notes on a notepad that you have with you at all times.

5. Indirect approach

Arrange for a group to get together. Approach a problem from a different angle by discussing a related subject — usually one of broad scope. Your group could create a new idea or a new direction of enquiry that could solve your problem in a way that would not be possible by discussing the problem directly. The indirect approach is particularly useful if an impasse has been reached and a new approach to the problem must be considered.

6. Encyclopedia approach

This technique involves extensive research into the subject. All the information available is accumulated and organised into categories. The material is then reviewed to extract the ideas that you wish to pursue. The encyclopedia approach is most suitable to a research and development organisation, or an individual with the time, personnel, and financial resources to perform the research.

7. Modifying components

This technique assumes that a new idea is merely the modification of an old idea. You start the process by choosing a product or service to improve. You then list all its parts and the features of each part. Next, in a systematic fashion, alter or modify the features better to meet the original purpose, to improve the product, or to satisfy a whole new purpose. This technique is a common form of organised thinking, and can produce many potential solutions or improvements.

8. Systematic analysis

In this approach, you attempt to discover all possible combinations of potential solutions to a problem. First identify the problem, then determine and list all its variables. Then list all possible ways of doing the job under each category of variable. Next, cut your list of variables and potential solutions into strips of paper. Now mix and match all the variables to create ideas or suggestions of ideas by examining each possible combination of variables. Systematic analysis will possibly assist in creating a whole new approach to the problem.

9. Meditation

There are various techniques for mental relaxation, confidence building, goal focusing and idea stimulation. Meditation techniques can sometimes provide these benefits as well as a mental environment to generate innovative thoughts. Check with your public library for books relating to meditation, and see if this approach works for you.

Tips for creative thinking

The process of creative thinking can create emotions ranging from elation to frustration. That is natural and to be expected. There are important steps to follow to try to minimise emotional frustration and maximise production. Maintaining a positive attitude is very important.

A summary of tips for successful creativity follows. Most of these tips are common sense, but anyone who has been involved in creative thinking knows that they are sometimes difficult to remember.

1. Keep your mind active and alert

Constantly assemble and evaluate information, think, and observe, to seek out new ideas or a new approach. Use and experiment with the creative techniques discussed earlier.

2. Use other resources

Don't rely only on your own perceptions and ideas. If you are stuck or want to expand your insight, consult an expert. You'll find them within the industry, at universities, and at private or public research institutions. Speak to the reference librarian at your public library.

3. Keep your goals in sight

It is important to use your goal as a point of reference, to act as a motivator, and to keep you on target. It also allows you to assess your progress and the accuracy of your projections.

4. Keep an open mind

Consider the alternatives to your approach. Don't have tunnel vision or develop a mental block when considering a new and different way of looking at things.

5. Don't deny reality

If you have looked at a concept with all its variations and possibilities, but keep coming to dead ends, maybe there is no solution. Maybe your approach needs to be changed. Don't continue on a particular course if it becomes clear that it is not working.

6. Take a rest when discouraged

If you find yourself becoming frustrated, angry, or discouraged, stop for a while. Leave the problem alone until you have regained your enthusiasm and perspective. Then you will be able to start again with new determination and a different approach.

7. Segment the problem

If you feel your problem is too complex or overwhelming, break it down into manageable pieces. Take a part of the problem and work on it one step at a time. Segmenting the problem will give you a feeling of accomplishment and open new perspectives. You will view the whole far more effectively after working successfully on its parts.

8. Work methodically

If you attempt to move too quickly, you could miss many important steps in the creative process, and get discouraged or fail in your objectives.

Summary of business ideas and preferences

Reflect on your thoughts and fantasies about the business

ideas that you have generated so far. Think of those that you now find challenging and would like to pursue further. Develop an updated list of these ideas, in random order.

_____

_____

_____

_____

_____

Next, make a master list of all the types of business that interest you. List them randomly at first, then go back and rank them by number.

_____

_____

_____

_____

_____

Chapter 5

Selecting the Right Business Opportunity

This chapter discusses criteria for analysing your business opportunities, how to shortlist your preferences, and the basic routes to business ownership.

Criteria for analysing your business possibilities

There are several criteria for analysing the businesses you are considering.

1. Personal capability assessment

Think about the personality traits required to succeed in the business you are considering. Reflect on your personal capability as identified in earlier exercises, and review your responses to Quizzes 1, 2 and 3 in Part 2.

2. Selection criteria

Figure 3 provides you with an analysis of the criteria required to meet your business objectives. Your decisions on these criteria will affect the way you work, your standard of living, your personal development and your business's geographical location. After you have obtained enough detailed information about the businesses you are considering, use the following guide to assist you in the screening process.

Complete Figure 5.1 now. Do *not* fill in the column on 'Degree of importance' at this time.

                                                    **Degree of
                                                    importance**

1. Amount of capital required
    - Total   _____   _____
    - Amount you are providing   _____   _____
    - Amount others are providing   _____   _____

2. Annual income needs   _____   _____

3. Business sector preferred (retail,
    service, wholesale, industrial,
    manufacturing, research and
    development)   _____   _____

4. Increase in net worth of
    business desired within three
    years (ie return on investment).
    (Express in percentage terms.)   _____   _____

5. Nature of work environment
    preferred (eg indoors/outdoors,
    manual/office, alone/with
    people). (List all preferences.)   _____   _____

6. Percentage of management you
    would prefer to provide
    personally   _____   _____

7. Percentage of personal inter-
    action preferred (eg with
    employees, suppliers,
    customers, retail sales)   _____   _____

8. Nature of long-term
    involvement (permanent
    full-time, eventual part-time,
    eventual absentee ownership)   _____   _____

9. Amount of status desired.
    (State low, medium, or high.)   _____   _____

10. Personal development (eg use
    skills and education, contribute
    something worthwhile and
    lasting to society, travel, see
    the world, and meet people).
    (Outline the motives that
    are important to you.)   _____   _____

Degree of importance

11. Size of business. (State the projected number of employees.) _____ _____

12. Hours of business (eg five days per week, Saturdays, Sundays, evenings, 40/60/ 70 or more hours per week). (State acceptable work-load.) _____ _____

13. Travel. (State acceptable amount of time spent away from home.) _____ _____

14. Degree of support from marriage partner required for approval of business venture. (State percentage.) _____ _____

15. Rate of business growth desired (eg slow — less than 10 per cent per year; moderate — 10 to 15 per cent per year; fast — over 20 per cent per year) _____ _____

16. Location. (State geographical area preferred.) _____ _____

17. Size of community preferred. (Estimate population.) _____ _____

18. Nature of community preferred (eg rural, industrial, recreational, maritime, ethnic) _____ _____

19. Commuting time to work accepted (eg over 1 hour, 30 minutes, less than 15 minutes) _____ _____

Figure 5.1 *Business selection guide*

The next step is to evaluate the degree of importance to you of each of the questions you have just answered. These personal preferences are a significant factor in selecting the business that is right for you.

Rate the business selection factors on a scale of importance from one to five. One indicates the factor is irrelevant, and five that the factor is of great importance. The other numbers represent relative importance in between. Write the value for degree of importance where indicated on Figure 5.1.

3. Assessment of current and future state of the business

The next assessment is whether or not the business being considered is viable. Various factors to be analysed include its current profitability, potential earnings, growth pattern, and the owner's reasons for selling. If you intend to start up a business, you should research other owners in the same type of business; ask why they are satisfied or whether they regret being in that business. This research can be done more easily outside your immediate geographical area to avoid competitors' resistance; ask in a town or city close by. Explain your reasons for the research candidly.

Screening your business possibilities

The screening process will allow you to separate serious possibilities from the tentative prospects listed at the beginning of this chapter. By the time you have completed the following steps, you will have a good basis for deciding which business or businesses best suit you.

1. Making the initial selection

List the businesses you ranked at the end of the last chapter across the top of Figure 5.2. Refer to your business selection criteria outlined in Figure 5.1. Then answer 'Yes' or 'No' on Figure 5.2 beside each of the 19 selection categories, depending on whether or not that business meets the criteria you have set. Add up the number of positive answers, and total them at the bottom. The businesses that score high should be considered more seriously and compared with each other. That will be done in the final selection analysis that follows.

Possible types of business:	1	2	3	4	5
Criteria	Yes/No	Yes/No	Yes/No	Yes/No	Yes/No
1. Capital required					
2. Income needs					
3. Business sector					
4. Return on investment					
5. Work environment					
6. Personal management					
7. Interaction with others					
8. Nature of long-term involvement					
9. Status desired					
10. Personal development					
11. Size of business					
12. Hours of business					
13. Travel away from home					
14. Support from marriage partner					
15. Rate of business growth					
16. Geographical location					
17. Size of community					
18. Nature of community					
19. Distance to work					
TOTALS					

Figure 5.2. *Assessing business selection*

Highest interest businesses:		1		2		3
Criteria	Yes	Degree of importance	Yes	Degree of importance	Yes	Degree of importance
1. Capital required	___	_____	___	_____	___	_____
2. Income needs	___	_____	___	_____	___	_____
3. Business sector	___	_____	___	_____	___	_____
4. Return on investment	___	_____	___	_____	___	_____
5. Work environment	___	_____	___	_____	___	_____
6. Personal management	___	_____	___	_____	___	_____
7. Interaction with others	___	_____	___	_____	___	_____
8. Nature of long-term involvement	___	_____	___	_____	___	_____
9. Status desired	___	_____	___	_____	___	_____
10. Personal development	___	_____	___	_____	___	_____
11. Size of business	___	_____	___	_____	___	_____
12. Hours of business	___	_____	___	_____	___	_____
13. Travel away from home	___	_____	___	_____	___	_____
14. Support from marriage partner	___	_____	___	_____	___	_____
15. Rate of business growth	___	_____	___	_____	___	_____
16. Geographical location	___	_____	___	_____	___	_____
17. Size of community	___	_____	___	_____	___	_____
18. Nature of community	___	_____	___	_____	___	_____
19. Distance to work	___	_____	___	_____	___	_____
IMPORTANCE VALUE TOTAL	___	_____	___	_____	___	_____

Figure 5.3. *Personal importance factor comparison*

2. Making the final selection

Refer to Figure 5.2 for the businesses that scored the highest. List these across the top of Figure 5.3. Then fill in only the 'Yes' answers that were given in Figure 5.2 beside the business selection criteria. Next, allocate the value given to each selection factor outlined in Figure 5.1. Write that number beside each 'Yes' answer in Figure 5.3. Total the numbers in each vertical column. This will give you a further basis for assessment. The higher the number, the closer the business meets your perceived needs and values, interests, and expertise.

4. Criteria for verifying your final selection

You have shortlisted your selection to a few good prospects. Before you go any further, ask at least two or three people who know you well to review your list of businesses. Ask them to give you their opinion of whether or not they think you are suited for these businesses, and if not, why not? You should also review your personal capability assessment to make sure your skills are relevant to the prospective business.

Quick ways to use the business selection guide

You can adapt the selection process to the amount of time available to you at any one time, and use it as a quick check for any business opportunity.

If you have only one hour to consider a business opportunity:

- fill in Figure 5.2
- fill in Figure 5.3, then
- determine whether or not the total importance value is worth your interest.

If you have only one day to consider the business opportunity:

- do all that you would do in the one-hour test
- compare the results with other business opportunities you are currently considering or have considered in the past

- compare the skills needed for this business opportunity with those in your personal capability assessment, then
- sleep on the idea overnight, and
- decide in the morning if you want to pursue the opportunity further.

If you have one month to consider the business opportunity:

- do all that you would do in the one-day test
- speak to owners of businesses like the one you are considering
- every week honestly reassess how you feel about the business opportunity
- speak to a solicitor and accountant if you are seriously interested, then
- at the end of the month, decide if you want to pursue the business opportunity further.

Basic routes to business ownership

Now that you have selected some serious business prospects, you have to decide the route you want to take to owning your own business. There are three basic routes: starting a new business, buying an existing one, or franchising.

1. Starting a new business

Starting a new business is often the most attractive choice for a beginner. The capital costs appear to be less and there's the satisfaction of bringing your very own enterprise into being. But against that must be balanced the extra time and effort, the special skills needed, the higher risk faced, and the losses or low income in the early stages.

There are only so many potential customers, and the new venture must attract and keep a large enough share to survive and prosper. That is possible only in the following limited situations:

(a) An existing business is poorly run in some obvious and critical way, and you can offer noticeably better service, product or prices, or market the firm more effectively.

(b) Your idea for a new service, product, or method of

      production or distribution is so different that direct competition from existing firms is minimal.

(c) The market is expanding, leaving room for another business without the pressure of cutting profit to compete with low prices. Also, new customers have no existing loyalties or buying habits to change.

(d) The market is fragmented among many small competitors. You could easily take a few customers from everyone.

(e) Customer loyalties and buying habits are not a factor; for example, in a direct mail business. You can start small and still be as efficient as competitors.

(f) Customer loyalty is important, and you presently work in the field and can take your clientele with you.

2. Buying an existing business

An alternative to starting your own business is to purchase an existing one. It offers the advantage of an existing customer base without adding to the competition. Earnings appear more quickly and financing may be easier, but you will pay extra for the goodwill you are buying.

The decision to buy a business can be one of the most critical in your life. Despite the risk, many people pursue this type of transaction without adequate investigation. Take time to obtain as much information as possible about the business. Often a buyer is tempted to make a quick offer for the business based on emotional, not objective reasons. Remember the effort required to earn the money you are investing, and realise the liabilities that could occur should the business fail.

It is important to investigate why the business is for sale. The seller may give ill health as the reason for selling, but the true reason may be declining business because of new competition, lack of customer demand, or some other reason. Although you may be convinced that with better management the business can be improved, in many cases you will be deceiving yourself.

Make certain you determine that the type and size of business you are thinking of buying is compatible with your talents, interests, personality and capital. Be sure that you can adequately finance the purchase of the business and allow for sufficient operating capital.

The only accurate method of evaluating the worth of a business is to estimate its future profit potential. It is immaterial how much time or money a previous owner has put into the business. You want to make sure that you can get a fair return for your investment. Refer to Appendix 2 for a checklist of questions you should ask before buying a business.

3. Franchising

Franchising is a licensing system in which a company, the franchisor, gives the franchise holder, or franchisee, the right to market a specific product or service in a defined territory. The franchisor usually retains control over how the product or service is merchandised.

Franchising should offer independent ownership while following proven management practices. The franchise holder thus benefits from the franchisor's experience and help in the choice of location, marketing, financing, record-keeping, and promotion. As a franchisee, you start out with an established reputation and name. Your business is organised and operated with the advantages of standardisation. The system generally offers real advantages as a means of owning your own business, but it cannot guarantee a profit. The franchisee, who maintains independence, is ultimately responsible for the business's success or failure. It makes sense, therefore, to know everything about the venture before you begin.

The franchise contract spells out the relationship between the franchisor and the franchisee. It tells what the franchisor will provide in the way of initial and continuing assistance, and also what the financial and operational contributions of the franchisee will be. All verbal promises made by each party should be written into the agreement, and the document should be checked by a solicitor to protect your interests.

Some franchisors do not charge a franchise fee and others charge many thousands of pounds. As a prospective franchisee you should be thoroughly familiar with what you are getting for your money. For example, the franchise fee might be for the use of the company name, business forms and operating methods, initial training, assistance in selecting a location, help finding financing, and expertise in getting the business started. When the franchisor provides ongoing assistance such as purchasing, business counselling, advertising, and accounting, you may be charged a monthly fee or a percentage of sales. Sometimes a percentage of profit figure is used, usually based on gross sales. Often franchisors will charge no monthly fees, but make their profits from the sale of stock purchased from them.

A franchisor may charge other fees, including a site evaluation fee if it is not included in the franchise fee, mark-up on supplies and equipment, interest if the franchisor is assisting with financing directly, and lease payments when the franchisor acts as the landlord. The potential franchisee should carefully assess each franchise cost for value received.

If you are evaluating the possibilities of purchasing a franchise there are many other considerations to be explored. Appendix 3 refers to the types of questions you should ask when evaluating a franchise opportunity.

In all three routes to business ownership, it is essential that you receive competent legal and financial advice before commiting yourself. There are many complex considerations and possible pitfalls that require an objective and thorough review.

Chapter 6

Selecting Your Partners or Management Team

This chapter covers the techniques for recruiting your business partners or management team, the types of relationship possible, the nature of partnership agreements and management contracts, and methods of determining the behaviour of different personalities. It also includes a potential partner analysis.

Sources

It is important to choose partners who complement your strengths and personality, both of which you have determined in earlier chapters. The intense pressures of business affect a partnership in complex ways and the relationship, therefore, is always being tested.

Here are some sources of potential partners you may wish to consider:

1. Friends

It is possible that you have friends who possess the talent and personality to be a productive member of your management team. Unfortunately, it is often difficult to assess their capabilities objectively, and after the business has commenced, and you find you have chosen poorly, you could lose a friendship that you value highly.

2. Relatives

Relatives can provide a good pool of financial resources and commitment to the success of the enterprise. You might also have a better feeling for their personalities rather than the personality of an outsider. There are many examples of family businesses that have prospered, in some cases passing from one generation to another. However, you must be prepared to assess objectively what benefit your relatives will bring to the business. If the relationship or business does not work out, hurt feelings or complete estrangement could occur, and all the attendant pain will remain within the family unit. Also, the difficulty of objectively evaluating their performance, and making difficult management decisions, could be impeded to the detriment of the business.

3. Former business associates

It is common for many businesses to be started by two or more partners who were formerly employees of the same firm. In this situation you probably have had an opportunity to objectively assess your ability to work with the others in a business setting.

4. Business consultants

You may wish to consider selecting a consultant as an adviser to your management team on a retainer or on request. Look in the Yellow Pages under consultants, management and business consultants, industrial consultants, and so on.

Consultants normally charge on an hourly or daily basis. Other forms of payment could be discussed, including an equity position in the company. But remember that a consultant is an independent contractor, not an employee, and generally does not perform advisory or management services on an exclusive basis, except for a specific period. At times, there is potential for conflict of interest if a consultant works for you and a competitor at the same time.

5. Spouse

If you decide to go into business with your spouse, be extremely careful and thoroughly examine the pitfalls in advance. It is important that you both do the exercises in this book so that you have an opportunity to discuss your areas of difference and agreement before you begin your venture together. Some husband and wife business combinations work extremely well. Others result in chronic conflict that hurts the marital and family relationship.

6. Competitors' employees

You may consider recruiting possible partners from the staff of competing businesses. The advantage of this approach is the benefit you obtain from someone who is knowledgeable in your business area and familiar with the market.

7. Classified ads

Local and financial newspapers are effective vehicles for finding potential partners. The classified sections comprise two categories:

(a) people who are looking for business opportunities and have the talent, qualifications, and/or money to invest, and

(b) people who are seeking other people with talent, qualifications, and/or money to invest.

You should thoroughly research the classified ads once you have identified the type of individual you are looking for. You should also consider placing an ad in the appropriate newspapers to find potential partners.

8. Professionals

Traditional business advisers (ie solicitors and accountants) should also be considered as possible partners. Professionals are frequently looking for possible investments. Their contribution of time or money should be quantified, and equity in the company negotiated accordingly. Generally, it is better to know the professional personally or have one referred to you by friends or associates.

9. Venture capitalists

You may wish to consider an investor as an equity partner in your business. The venture capitalist may or may not play an active role in day-to-day management, but will monitor the ongoing operation of the business closely.

Venture capitalists are very selective of their partnerships and joint venture relationships. They tend to be very sophisticated and cautious about the risks of new businesses. Adequate capital, a detailed and realistic business plan, and a balanced management team with expertise will be convincing considerations for the venture capitalist.

113

Partners and shareholders

As mentioned earlier, it is not uncommon to have disputes among partners, whether they are actual partners or act as shareholders in a corporation. Conflict is likely to occur when two or more people share decision-making responsibilities, but have incompatible dreams, goals, and expectations. Consequently, self-interest often dictates decision-making, rather than the interests of the business. Personality and behaviour differences, as well as skill deficiencies, can also contribute to problems.

To avoid these problems, you should have any potential partner complete the management skills test in Quiz 3, in Part 2 of this book. Also, Quiz 4 on page 121 provides a further basis for partner analysis.

You should also plan for all possibilities by considering and negotiating agreements that spell out the procedures to be followed in the event of a disagreement. All agreements and contracts should be in writing.

Partnership agreement

A partnership agreement is advisable in any partnership. It normally outlines what each partner contributes to the business, be it financial, material, or managerial. In general, the partnership agreement defines the role of each partner in the business relationship. Some of the typical articles contained in a partnership agreement are shown in Figure 6.1.

If you are considering partnership, think about each article in Figure 6.1, then see your solicitor to draw up the papers.

Shareholders' agreement

Many shareholders believe that company bylaws set out the recipe for resolving problems within the company and between the shareholders, directors, and officers. In most cases the bylaws only cover formulas for resolving disputes in a few circumstances. It is the shareholders' agreement that expands the protection to resolve fairly any disputes between shareholders.

If you intend to incorporate and have one or more

1. Name, purpose and location of partnership
2. Duration of agreement
3. Financial contribution by partners
4. Role of individual partners in business management
5. Authority of partner in conduct of business
6. Nature and degree of each partner's contribution to the business
7. How business expenses will be handled
8. Separate debts
9. Signing of cheques and management of bank account
10. Division of profits and losses
11. Preparation of accounts and recording systems
12. Drawings or salaries
13. Absence and disability
14. Death of a partner (dissolution and winding up)
15. Rights of the continuing partner
16. Sale of partnership interest
17. Settlement of disputes and arbitration
18. Additions, alterations, or modifications to partnership agreement

Figure 6.1. *Checklist of articles in a partnership agreement*

shareholders in your corporation, it would be wise to obtain your solicitor's advice on a shareholders' agreement to protect your interests.

A shareholders' agreement involves the same concepts of protection as a partnership agreement. Many of the provisions outlined in the partnership agreement are also included in the shareholders' agreement. There are additional provisions frequently covered in the shareholders' agreement including the following:

(a) A restriction on transfer of shares
(b) A purchase agreement that sets out the formula for buying or selling shares in the company
(c) A forced buy-out provision

    (d) Liability for past debtors and creditors

    (e) A provision on repayment of shareholders' loans by the company.

Management agreement

In a situation where one of the partners, shareholders, or directors is also acting in a managerial position or as an employee in some other capacity, it is advisable to have the relationship detailed in writing for the protection of both the individual and the company. The contract should cover duties and responsibilities, salary, commissions, bonuses and a basis for their variation and the term of employment.

If a partner, shareholder, or director is being employed in other than a managerial capacity (for example, as a commission salesperson), it is important to consider an employment contract at the outset. The employment contract covers many of the same clauses in the management contract referred to above.

Consulting contract

When you decide to employ a consultant, whether on an ongoing basis or on request, you should establish a consulting contract setting out the nature of the advisory relationship, the costs involved, the nature of payment, and the duration of the contract.

Determining your personality and style

Understanding your own personality and style, and that of your potential partners or management team, is very important. You want to make sure your style and theirs complement, not conflict with, each other. You want to make sure your potential partner's style will benefit your business.

The following exercises outline styles of behaviour based on four commonly recognised personalities; they are general guides only. It is a helpful exercise to rate yourself as honestly and accurately as you can on Figure 6.2. The horizontal gradient relates to how passive or aggressive you perceive yourself, and the vertical gradient relates to how

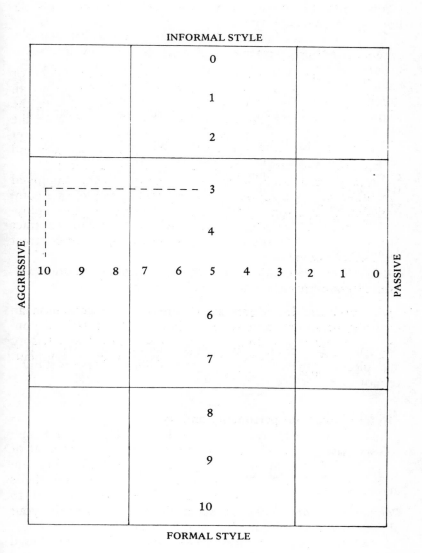

Figure 6.2. *Personality behavioural gradient*

informal or formal you see yourself. When making your rating, think of yourself in your work environment, not at home or in a social setting.

Once you have marked horizontal and vertical planes, extend two lines outwards and mark where they intersect in one of the four quadrants (the dotted line shows an example). Now have two other people, who you believe know you well within the job context, rate you using the same figure without any of your marks on it. Average the three assessments.

Now refer to Figure 6.3. This figure shows how people tend to behave in blended styles, rather than as extremes of one of the four distinct styles. Transfer your average mark from Figure 6.2 to the same point of Figure 6.3 to identify your typical style of behaviour.

The four common personality styles are as follows:

1. Supporters

Traits. Sensitive, gentle, approachable, easygoing, emotionally honest, good listeners, understanding, caring.

Special talents. Supporters allow others a protective, loving environment in which to be themselves.

Perception by others. Easygoing, friendly, eager to please and pleasant; may also be seen as unwilling to take a stand, unmotivated, or overly yielding.

2. Analysers

Traits. Committed, loyal, efficient, dedicated, good problem-solvers, wise.

Special talents. Analysers contribute justice, order, wisdom and excellence.

Perception by others. Expert, steady, knowledgeable, dependable and not easily upset; may also be seen as tedious, boring, uncommunicative, and incapable of making a decision.

3. Promoters

Traits. Active, energetic, relaxed, creative, friendly, fun-loving, have positive attitude, a good leader.

INFORMAL STYLE

Promoter		Supporter	
Promoter	Promoter	Supporter	Supporter
Promoter	Supporter	Promoter	Supporter
Promoter	Promoter	Supporter	Supporter
Controller	Analyser	Controller	Analyser
Controller		**Analyser**	
Controller	Controller	Analyser	Analyser
Promoter	Supporter	Promoter	Supporter
Controller	Controller	Analyser	Analyser
Controller	Analyser	Controller	Analyser

AGGRESSIVE

PASSIVE

FORMAL STYLE

Figure 6.3. *Personality behavioural matrix*

119

Special talents. Promoters express enthusiasm, and encourage and elicit it in others.

Perception by others. Fun-loving, exciting, provocative, energetic and personable; may also be seen as disorganised, emotional, pushy, loud, erratic, or approval seeking.

4. Controllers

Traits. Ambitious, self-confident, competent, responsible, independent, lead by example, precise.

Special talents. Controllers provide guidance, inspiration and leadership.

Perception by others. Cool, efficient, organised, competent, knowledgeable and in control; may also be seen as power driven, arrogant, egotistic, cold, and inflexible.

Now that you have a better understanding of these styles, rate your potential partners or management team within the job context. You want to make sure that your behavioural styles do not interfere with the productive and profitable management of your business.

Having a business team that balances the needs of the venture is essential. For example, if you have defined yourself as a 'promoter/promoter' and there are two other potential partners with the same behavioural styles, you may have future business problems unless there is an extended management team to provide a balance.

Complete Quiz 4 when you have shortlisted your potential partners.

Potential Partner Analysis Quiz

The following questionnaire should be completed by you about your prospective business partner. It should also be completed by your prospective business partner about you. The next step is to exchange your answers, and discuss areas where your answers conflict, or where sensitive concerns have been raised.

It is essential that you be completely candid in your responses. With the pressures of the business relationship, you will soon discover the real problem areas when working together. By that time it may be too late to do anything about it without a lot of pain and expense. It makes sense to identify and resolve areas of conflict *before* you start the business. If you can't resolve the outstanding issues, don't go into business together.

Tick each question in the column that most accurately expresses your opinion. The responses range from 'strongly yes' (column A) to 'strongly no' (column F). If the answer is unknown or unimportant to you, tick column G. Answer every question.

Section 1. Questionnaire

	A	B	C	D	E	F	G
1. Do you trust your business partner in all areas of the business?	___	___	___	___	___	___	___
2. Does your partner trust you in all areas of the business?	___	___	___	___	___	___	___
3. Do you and your business partner have the same or similar financial goals for the business?	___	___	___	___	___	___	___

121

	A	B	C	D	E	F	G

4. Does your business partner have the same or similar expectations for the business as you do:
   (a) in the first six months? ___ ___ ___ ___ ___ ___ ___
   (b) in the first year? ___ ___ ___ ___ ___ ___ ___
   (c) in the first three years? ___ ___ ___ ___ ___ ___ ___
   (d) in the first five years? ___ ___ ___ ___ ___ ___ ___

5. Does your business partner have skills in areas where you are weak? ___ ___ ___ ___ ___ ___ ___

6. Is your business partner as committed to the business idea as you are? ___ ___ ___ ___ ___ ___ ___

7. Do you think your business partner would stay with the business even though he or she might not receive his or her salary, or draw when expected, or if external obstacles to business success arise? ___ ___ ___ ___ ___ ___ ___

8. Does your business partner have capital or access to capital for investing in the business? ___ ___ ___ ___ ___ ___ ___

9. Is your business partner willing to perform whatever menial tasks might be required to get the job done? ___ ___ ___ ___ ___ ___ ___

10. Does your business partner have good people skills? ___ ___ ___ ___ ___ ___ ___

11. To the best of your knowledge, is your business partner emotionally stable? ___ ___ ___ ___ ___ ___ ___

12. To the best of your knowledge, is your business partner financially stable? ___ ___ ___ ___ ___ ___ ___

13. Is your business partner innovative and open to new ideas? ___ ___ ___ ___ ___ ___ ___

14. Might your partner get tired of the business and want to sell it in two years or so? ___ ___ ___ ___ ___ ___ ___

	A	B	C	D	E	F	G

15. Is your business partner expecting to make a modest financial return, rather than making a lot of money?

16. Is your business partner interested in a serious long-term commitment, rather than just helping you get started?

17. Does your business partner have a background in accounting or financial management?

18. Does your business partner have enough genuine regard for you still to respect you as a person, even if the business partnership does not materialise after you have gone through this mutual assessment exercise?

19. Do you feel confident that your business partner does not feel pressured into coming into the business relationship with you?

20. Are you intending to have a solicitor draw up a legal partnership agreement or shareholders' agreement?

21. If your prospective business partner is your son or daughter, will you give him or her the full responsibilities of a partner, with benefits?

22. If your business partner is your spouse, will he or she be paid a fee or salary for his or her work?

23. If your business partner is your spouse, will he or she have to leave a job to work with you?

24. Is your business partner resourceful?

25. Is your business partner flexible?

	A	B	C	D	E	F	G
26. Is your business partner a skilful organiser?	—	—	—	—	—	—	—
27. Is your business partner an objective decision-maker?	—	—	—	—	—	—	—
28. Does your business partner delegate responsibilities easily?	—	—	—	—	—	—	—
29. Will your business partner willingly put in the long hours necessary to make the business venture succeed?	—	—	—	—	—	—	—
30. Will your business partner agree to signing a legal partnership agreement or shareholders' agreement?	—	—	—	—	—	—	—
31. Is your business partner in good physical health?	—	—	—	—	—	—	—
32. Is your business partner self-confident?	—	—	—	—	—	—	—
33. Does your business partner have perseverance?	—	—	—	—	—	—	—

Section 2. Additional questions

Now answer the following questions:

1. Why do you believe your business partner is compatible with you?

_____

_____

_____

_____

2. What are your business partner's best assets and capabilities that will help your business?

_____

_____

_____

3. What are your business partner's areas of weakness that could have a negative effect on your business unless corrected?

_____

_____

_____

_____

4. How long have you known your business partner and under what circumstances?

_____

_____

_____

_____

5. If your partner is a spouse or relative, what effect do you believe it will have on your personal relationship if the business fails?

_____

_____

_____

_____

6. What kind of partnership benefit are you willing to give your business partner?

_____

_____

_____

_____

7. What kind of partnership benefit will your business partner expect or require?

_____

_____

_____

_____

8. Could you operate the business without your business partner, and how would you compensate?

_____
_____
_____
_____

9. Could your business partner operate the business without you, and if so how would he or she compensate?

_____
_____
_____
_____

10. Does your partner have skills in areas in which you are weak, and if so, what are those areas?

_____
_____
_____
_____

Now that you have completed the questionnaire, go over the questions in Section 1. You should reassess and discuss the issues covered in the questions if your answers or your partner's answers do not fall into columns 'A' or 'B'. The closer the answers are to 'F', the more concern you should have. Any responses in category 'G' (unknown) should be thoroughly discussed as the issues raised have to be clarified and resolved to your mutual satisfaction.

The questions in Section 2 will give you the basis for further serious review and reflection.

Chapter 7

Selecting Your Business and Professional Advisers

You should consider the need for an extended management team to advise your business in specialised areas where you lack knowledge, ability, or interest. Your advisers are, in effect, your employees and associates, and should be considered an integral part of management decision-making. Even though you may have partners who will assist in the management of your business, outside advisers are very important.

Every business decision involves a legal decision or implication. Every business decision involves accounting, bookkeeping and, at times, tax considerations. The fatality rate of small businesses is enormously high. Statistically, the odds are approximately ten to one that you, as a small business person, will not be in business five years after you begin your venture.

This chapter discusses the benefits of the effective use of business and professional advisers, how to evaluate them, and how to use their skills to your advantage.

General criteria

How well you select your professional and business advisers will have a direct bearing on the success of your business. Poor advisers or no advisers at all will almost certainly lead to your business downfall. Your main advisers are your solicitor and accountant, followed by your bank manager. You should see at least three different people from each of these three areas before you make your selection as it is important to have a comparative assessment.

The following general guidelines should assist you in the careful search and selection of your advisers.

1. Recommendations

One of the most reliable methods of finding an adviser is by personal recommendation from your bank, your existing advisers or friends in business whose judgement and business sense you trust. Banks and business advisers who deal on a regular basis with professional advisers are in a good position to make judgements based on their business dealings. When solicitors, accountants or banks refer each other, it implies a good working relationship and mutual trust. Don't rely completely on any recommendation; make your own cautious assessment.

2. Credentials

Anyone can call himself an accountant in the UK but only qualified accountants are eligible to audit the accounts of limited companies. A qualified accountant will belong to a professional body and have letters after his name: ACA or FCA, and in Scotland, CA, designate members of the respective Institute of Chartered Accountants. Members of the Chartered Association of Certified Accountants have ACCA or FCCA. Accountants may also be members of the Chartered Institute of Finance and Accountancy and the Chartered Institute of Management Accountants but few members of these bodies will be found in accountancy practices.

Certification and credentials only ensure that the individual has passed a minimum standard of education. They do not ensure that the person is a dynamic, innovative, or creative business adviser with a specific amount of experience relevant to your needs.

3. Clientele

Most professional advisers have a homogeneous client base. Some advisers have many small business clients, some emphasise personal clients, while others go after corporate business. An adviser with a good base of small to medium-size commercial clients will probably be the most suited to your business needs.

4. Fees

Fees vary according to the size of the community in which

the professional practises, the size of the practice, and the volume of business. You may find that advisers who charge fees at the middle to high end of the scale are often excellent practitioners in high demand who are still aggressive and innovative in their business practice. Advisers at the low end of the fee scale may be entrepreneurial types, but cut-rate pricing may also indicate a cut-rate, high-volume approach to business that will not suit your objectives. Low prices sometimes indicate low quality, low esteem, or little experience. Very high priced advisers tend to be more conservative, less aggressive and less willing to spend the necessary time with small business clients, as their priorities are the big firms. Fees vary and many professionals will negotiate them.

In a small or medium-size community, a realistic hourly rate for a partner's time is approximately £35 per hour, and £25 per hour for a legal executive. Correspondence and phone calls are charged extra.

5. Technical competence

You must be satisfied that your adviser is competent in the areas of your greatest need. Ask him or her how experienced and how comfortable he or she is in your field. A specific understanding of your type of business can enable your advisers to provide the exact assistance you require. This is different from competence at a technical skill. It has more to do with experience in a particular industry. If the adviser has provided guidance to other similar small businesses, there is an increased possibility that the adviser will be able to provide you with more reliable assistance.

6. Style and personality

A critical factor in the selection of advisers, beyond simple compatibility, is style. You can have greater confidence in the aggressive adviser who takes the initiative and offers advice before you request it. This style indicates an initiator rather than a reactor, a person who anticipates and performs before matters become serious. It also indicates a creator, an entrepreneur, and a person who can empathise with your problems and concerns. This kind of adviser is more likely to come up with creative solutions to problems, and be a complement to your planning function. This type of adviser

129

will be not only a sounding board, but a true part of the management team.

7. Confidence

You should feel a sense of confidence when dealing with your adviser, both generally and when working together on a specific problem. Confidence will exist when you have a certain amount of personal compatibility with your adviser. If you don't, you will probably end up rejecting a fair amount of advice. In other words, if you do not feel that good chemistry exists between you and your adviser, seek a replacement as soon as possible.

Never allow your advisers to treat you in a condescending or paternalistic manner. You should consider them as equals offering a service of their special knowledge.

8. Communication

You should select an adviser who communicates openly, and free of jargon. Your adviser should explain the necessary concepts to you so that you understand the issues involved and the decisions that have to be made. Effective communication also means that your advisers forward to you any correspondence relating to your business sent or received through their offices.

9. Commitment

It is important to sense that your adviser is committed to your best interests and your success. An adviser who is involved with larger, more important or higher paying clients than you may become indifferent to your needs. You should be alert to this.

10. Availability

It is important for your advisers to be available when you need them. You are spending time and money to develop a relationship that will enhance your business decisions. If your adviser is frequently out of town or, in the case of a solicitor, in court on a regular basis, you may not have the immediate access you need. Of course, if the adviser is of exceptional quality and ideally suited to your type of practice, some allowances should be made.

11. Length of time in practice

There is a natural correlation between degree of expertise and length of time in practice. Therefore, you should ask directly how many years' experience your adviser has in the area of your needs.

12. Ability to aid growth

A good professional adviser will have a history of assisting growth in other clients. The adviser should be able to anticipate growth problems in advance, and provide guidance to deal with them.

13. Size of firm

Choosing a small or large firm is, in many ways, a question of your personal style. Larger firms tend to be in the city centre. Their fees are higher and, generally, they do not have an orientation to small business in their marketing and service priorities. However, the larger firms do have highly specialised advisers and a referral base of associate personnel. This degree of specialisation may or may not be necessary in your situation. It is not uncommon in larger firms to have small business clients passed over to junior associates or students in training, while the more senior advisers handle larger clients.

Smaller firms generally relate well to small business entrepreneurs. Selecting an adviser in a small or medium-size firm of three to ten people provides you with alternative advisers if you need them. A sole practitioner may be very busy, too generalised in his or her areas of practice, and lack the referral base within the firm.

Choosing a solicitor

There are basically two types of solicitor that you should consider as your advisers. The same person might be able to assume both roles.

First, you need a solicitor who specialises in small businesses. One who cares about small business clients assumes the same role and attitude towards your business health and survival that your doctor does to your physical health.

Second, you need a solicitor who specialises in contract law. You may need to have several standard contracts prepared depending upon the type and style of business you are considering. There will be times when you will need to have a specialised contract made up by a solicitor, or have your solicitor review and advise you on a contract that a client has prepared.

If your business solicitor is not expert in contract law, request a referral to someone within the firm or outside who is. For continuity and efficiency, you will want to maintain him or her for all matters that don't require additional expertise. You should be able to phone your solicitor as the need arises, and feel confident that the unique aspects of your business are known and understood.

For your protection, you should engage a solicitor before you start up your business, as there are many legal pitfalls that can be encountered. There is a temptation to save money on legal fees in the early stages of the business when cash flow is minimal. Some people do their own incorporation to save on initial start-up expenses, but then continue the saving by never obtaining legal or accounting advice: an unfortunate example of false economy and bad judgement.

Choosing an accountant

An accountant is the other essential business adviser on your management team. It is very important that you obtain a qualified accountant. A bookkeeper is *not* an accountant and there is no law to prevent anyone using the name 'accountant' and purporting to provide accounting services without any qualifications or training. Make sure you check for professional designations. However, a *chartered* accountant can advise on all start-up procedures for a new business, including the tax and accounting considerations of various types of business organisation. An accountant will communicate with or coordinate work with your solicitor, if required. The accountant considers such important matters as when your business year-end should be and what books should be kept.

An accountant can advise you on preparing a business plan for a loan application. This includes recommending the type of loan you should consider and how it will be repaid. Documents such as a profit and loss account, a balance sheet and a financial statement can be prepared by the accountant. He or she may refer you to a bank, which can have a positive effect on your loan application if the bank knows and respects the accountant.

An accountant can advise on all aspects of tax planning and tax-related business decisions that occur from time to time and submit your tax returns to the Inland Revenue.

An accountant can also advise how to set up your office bookkeeping system. The accountant can have the book-keeping done by someone in his or her firm at a negotiated fee, or you can engage an independent bookkeeper.

An accountant can analyse and interpret your financial information, point out areas that need control, and recommend ways of implementing the necessary change.

An accountant may be aware of various government schemes that could be of interest to you.

An accountant can coordinate your personal and business affairs, and advise you on investments, tax, and other matters.

An accountant can advise and assist you if you want to change your proprietorship or partnership into a limited company.

Choosing a bank

Your relationship with your bank and bank manager is your financial lifeline. The process of selecting a bank is critical and comparative shopping is necessary to obtain the best combination of personality and knowledge.

The qualifications of the bank manager should be considered along with his or her specific experience with your type of business, reputation for taking risk, and the demands for security and reporting results.

Find out the amount of the bank's loan approval limit. If your needs are less than the limit, the loan can be approved by that individual without further review by a higher authority. This means you have to convince only one person to approve your loan request, not additional anonymous people behind the scenes. How well your relationship develops with the banker and how successfully your loans are approved will depend largely on the factors outlined in Chapter 9 on how to obtain financing.

There are dangers in your bank's relationship with you. When the manager changes, there is always a period of risk and uncertainty. The new manager may not want to have any medium or high risk loans on the books to taint his or her record. During the first three or four months after a new manager takes over, outstanding loans are reviewed and categorised within the criteria set by the new manager. This is the time when loans can be called in, additional security requested, or interest rates increased. You should develop a personal relationship with the manager when you take out a loan. If you hear that a new manager has taken over, make a point of introducing yourself quickly and briefly discuss your business in a positive way.

Bank policies change from time to time and your type of business could be looked upon as increasing in risk. For example, if property is in a slump in your area, a bank may decide to be very cautious about existing or pending loans related to it. If you are a property developer, that decision could affect your loan. If you think the bank is concerned about the risk involved in your business, prepare a realistic assessment of how you intend to deal with the situation in advance. You may have a diversified business, not just related to property, or you may have other options available that you could explain to your bank manager.

Choosing consultants

Private consultants

You may wish to approach a practising consultant for advice to assist you in your business. Consultants are not restrictively licensed like other professionals. To protect yourself, you should enquire about their expertise, qualifications, and length of experience. Obtain references and contact them.

Apply the general criteria for adviser selection. You will want to satisfy yourself that the consultant is personally sucessful. If the consultant has not been successful, how can he or she possibly offer advice that will help you towards success?

Consultants subsidised by government

Several government agencies have responsibility for giving advice to people wishing to start new businesses, or those whose businesses are undergoing problems of survival or growth. The first counselling session is free and a modest charge is made for later meetings.

The main agencies are:

(a) The Small Firms Service of the Department of Employment. To make contact, telephone the operator on 100 and ask for Freefone Enterprise.

(b) The Council for Small Industries in Rural Areas (CoSIRA) offers counselling sessions for businesses in English communities of under 10,000 inhabitants. Its counterparts in Scotland and Wales are The Scottish Development Agency and the Welsh Development Agency respectively.

There are over 200 Local Development Agencies and Local Enterprise Agencies in the UK. A complete list of their names and addresses may be obtained from Business in the Community at 227A City Road, London EC1V 1LX. All other relevant names and addresses are given in Appendix 4.

Chapter 8

Legal Forms of Business Structure

There are basically four forms of legal business structure: sole trader, partnership, cooperative, and limited company. You should seek competent legal and accounting advice before deciding on your business structure, as there could be distinct advantages or disadvantages to each depending upon your situation.

Many businesses start out as a sole trader, as that is the easiest way to start a business. A partnership consists of two or more people. Forming a limited company is a third option. The limited company can be owned by just one person (similar to a proprietorship), or two or more people (similar to a partnership). A cooperative is owned and controlled by those who work in it and membership is usually open to all employees. Each member will have one vote only, irrespective of the number of shares he or she owns. Cooperatives are usually registered as either a limited company, or as an industrial and provident society with the Registrar of Friendly Societies.

This chapter discusses the factors that you should examine when making a decision about your business structure.

Sole trader

A sole trader's business is owned by one person. It can be operated by one or more people. To establish yourself as a sole trader, you need only obtain whatever local licences or permissions you require and open your business. It is the simplest form of business structure and operation.

Advantages

Ease of formation. There is less formality and few legal restrictions associated with setting up as a sole trader. You can start almost immediately. There are no complex forms to complete and no documentation required between yourself and any other party. All that is legally necessary to operate is to register the business with the Inland Revenue and obtain any necessary licences or permits.

Cost. Registering the business involves minimal costs. There are no partnership or corporate agreements required because you are the sole owner.

Lack of complexity. A sole tradership is straightforward. Unlike other forms of business, there is little government control and, accordingly, no records to be filed. The owner and the business are taxed as one by the Inland Revenue.

Decision-making process. Decisions are made exclusively by the sole owner, who has complete authority and freedom to move. The owner does not have to obtain approval from partners, shareholders, or a board of directors.

Sole ownership of profits. The proprietor does not have to share the profits with anyone. The profits generated by the business belong to one person. The sole owner decides how and when the money will come out of the business.

Ease of terminating on sale of business. Apart from legal responsibilities to employees, creditors or perhaps customers or clients, you can sell the business or close it down at your will.

Flexibility. You are able to respond quickly to business needs in day-to-day management decisions as governed by the law and common sense.

Disadvantages

Unlimited liability. The sole owner's personal assets, such as house, property, car and investments, are liable to be seized, if necessary, to pay for outstanding business debts or liabilities. As mentioned earlier, the proprietor and the business are deemed to be one and the same in law.

Less financing capacity. It is more difficult for a proprietor to borrow money than for a partnership with various partners or a company with a number of major shareholders. A lender, when looking for security and evidence of outside resources, can turn to the other partners or shareholders connected with the business rather than just the one person in a proprietorship. A company can give an investor some form of equity position, which is not available in a proprietorship.

Unstable duration of business. The business might be crippled or terminated upon the illness or death of the owner. If no one is designated to take over the business, it may have to be sold or liquidated. Such an unplanned action may result in a loss.

Sole decision-making. In partnerships or limited companies, generally there is shared decision-making. In a proprietorship, just one person is involved, and if that person lacks business ability or experience, poor decision-making can cause the business to suffer.

Partnership

A partnership is usually defined as an association of two or more persons to carry on a business in common with a view to making a profit. The partnership is created by a contract, either verbal or written, between the individual parties, or can achieve legal status through long practice, in the absence of an agreement.

Advantages

Ease of formation. Legal formalities and expenses in forming a partnership are few compared with incorporation.

Pride of ownership and direct rewards. Pride of ownership generates personal motivation and identification with the business. The profit motive could be reinforced with more people having a vested interest.

Availability of more capital. A partnership can pool the funds of a number of people compared with a sole owner who has only his or her own resources to draw upon, unless loans are obtained.

138

Combination of expertise and talents. Two or more partners, by combining their energies and talents, can often be successful where one person alone would fail. This is particularly true if the business demands a variety of talents such as technical knowledge, sales ability, and financial skills. It is important that working partners bring complementary skills to the business, thereby reducing the workload of each partner.

Flexibility. A partnership may be relatively more flexible in the decision-making process than a limited company.

Disadvantages

Unlimited liability. The major disadvantage of a partnership is unlimited liability. All the partners are individually *and* collectively liable for all the debts of the partnership. Each partner's personal assets are liable to be seized if necessary to pay for outstanding business debts. This unlimited liability can be much more serious than the liability of a proprietorship.

Unstable duration of business. Any change in the partnership, such as the death of a partner, or the admission or withdrawal of a partner, changes the balance and may even terminate the partnership. These possibilities should be provided for in the partnership agreement.

Management difficulties. As mentioned, when more than one owner assumes responsibility for business management there is a possibility that differences of style, priorities and philosophy will arise. If these differences become serious disputes and are unresolvable, the partnership may have to be terminated, with all the financial and personal upset involved. It is difficult for future partners to foresee whether or not personalities and methods of operating will clash.

Relative difficulty in obtaining large capital sums. This is particularly true of long-term financing when compared with a limited company.

Partnership agreement problems. The larger a partnership becomes, the more complex the written agreement has to be to protect the rights and identify the responsibilities of each partner. This can result in additional administration and legal costs.

Difficulty·of disposing of partnership interests. To withdraw capital from the business requires approval from all the other partners. That takes time and involves legal and administrative expenses.

Limited company

A limited company is a legal entity, with share capital, that can be established by one or more individuals or other legal entities. It exists independently of these individuals or other legal entities.

Advantages

Limited liability of shareholders. Shareholders' personal assets are separate from the business and cannot be seized to pay for any outstanding business debts incurred by the company. There are exceptions, primarily related to the issue of fraud and directors' personal guarantees.

Corporate management flexibility. The owner or owners can be active in the management of the business to any degree they desire. Agents, officers and directors with specific authority can be appointed to manage the business. Employees can be given stock options to share in the ownership, which can increase incentive and interest.

Financing more readily available. Investors find it more attractive to invest in a limited company with its limited liability, than to invest in a business that could involve them to an extent greater than the amount of the investment. Long-term financing from lending institutions is more available since lenders may use both corporate assets and personal guarantees as security.

Continuous existence of the company. A company continues to exist and operate regardless of changes in the shareholders. Death of a shareholder does not discontinue the life of the company. Continuous existence is also an effective device for building and retaining goodwill.

Ownership is readily transferable. It is relatively simple to transfer ownership by share transfer unless there are corporate restrictions to the contrary.

Draws on expertise and skills of more than one individual. This feature is the same concept as in a partnership, where more partners, in this case shareholders, contribute diverse talents. However, a limited company is not required to have more than one shareholder.

Disadvantages

Extensive government regulations. More regulations affect a limited company than a sole proprietorship or partnership.

Manipulation. Minority shareholders can potentially be exploited by the decisions of the majority of the company.

Expense. It is more expensive to establish and operate a limited company because of the additional documents and forms that are required compared with a sole proprietorship or partnership.

Note: If there is more than one shareholder, a shareholders' agreement and management contract should be seriously considered (see Chapter 6). The selection of a potential partner or shareholder is covered in Chapter 6 and Quiz 4.

Corporate purposes

The Memorandum and Articles of Association set out the purposes of the company. When you list the purposes of the company, make sure that you define them expansively. Do not restrict the activity of your company. A general clause should be included allowing the corporation to expand into any business activity permitted by law. A competent solicitor can assist you in drawing this up.

Directors' responsibilities

Directors have legal responsibility for the proper running of their company; they are not responsible for dishonest co-directors unless they knew them to be acting dishonestly. Each director is personally liable to the company and to shareholders for anything he does which is not permitted under the Memorandum and Articles of Association and for anything done without reference to the company. If a director is negligent or dishonest with fraudulent intent, then he is responsible for any consequential loss caused to the company. The penalty in law may be a fine and/or imprisonment.

Directors have responsibilities to carry out the provisions of the Companies Act, and any legislation connected with employment, industrial training, health and safety.

Close companies

A close company is one which is controlled by up to five 'participants' and their 'associates', usually family and director-controlled companies. The controlling director is assumed by the Inland Revenue to run the company through his participants and associates.

Chapter 9

Financing

You will want to be familiar with the types of financing available, the various sources, how to approach financial lending institutions, and the type of security that may be required. You should also be aware of the reasons lending institutions or investors may turn down a request for funding. These matters and other issues will be covered in this chapter.

Types of financing

There are two basic types of financing: equity and debt.

1. Equity financing

The money that *you* put into a company or business is equity. Initially all money must come from your own resources, such as savings, or personal borrowing from financial institutions, friends, relatives, or business associates. As time progresses, retained earnings in the business will increase your equity.

If you have formed a limited company, you can buy one or more shares and lend the rest of the money to the company as a shareholder's loan. The advantages of a shareholder's loan are as follows:

(a) Lenders consider these loans as equity as long as the money is left in the company.

(b) It is easier to repay the loan than sell shares back to the company or to other investors.

(c) Interest may be paid. For example, if you or your friends would like to earn a return on your investment, an interest rate may be established. The alternative

143

is to pay dividends on shares when funds are available.
(d) Interest is tax deductible to the company.
(e) The loan can be repaid in part or full without tax consequences to the recipient, but investors under the Business Expansion Scheme must observe its conditions for repayment to benefit from tax concessions.

2. Debt financing

A debt is a loan. It must be repaid and the lender will charge interest on the money you have borrowed. With borrowed money, normally the principal and interest are paid back on a fixed monthly payment. You therefore have to include the principal and interest payments in a current business plan. Various forms of debt financing are discussed below.

(a) Short-term or operating loan (demand loan)
Short-term or operating loans are used for financing inventory, debtors, special purposes or promotions, and other items requiring working capital during peak periods.

The main sources of short-term loans are commercial banks or other financial institutions. Using a short-term loan is a good way to establish credit with a bank. This type of loan can be unsecured, or secured by your personal or business assets.

Short-term loans are usually negotiated for specific periods of time: 30, 60, or 90 days, and frequently for periods of up to a year or more. They may be repayable in a lump sum at the end of the period or in periodic instalments, such as monthly.

Other characteristics include:

- interest rate at time of signing lower than a term loan,
- fluctuating interest rate,
- repayment of the loan can be demanded at any time by the lender; usually only occurs when the account does not perform satisfactorily or when there is serious deterioration in the affairs of the business, and
- often obtained more quickly than a term loan.

(b) Overdraft
An overdraft is an agreement between you and the bank, specifying the maximum amount of overdraft the bank will

allow you at any one time for general operating purposes.

Overdrafts are usually established for one-year periods, subject to annual renegotiation and renewal. Other characteristics include:

- loan funds increase and decrease as you need the money,
- available from most banks,
- fluctuating interest rate,
- interest rate at time of signing may be lower than a term loan,
- the lender uses your debtors, the money owed to you by customers, and stock as security; for accounts due, the lender may lend between 50 and 75 per cent of the value, not including any amounts over 90 days; for stock, a lender may lend up to 50 per cent.
- can often be obtained more quickly than a term loan,
- repayment of the loan can be demanded at any time by the lender, or the level of credit reduced; usually only occurs when the account does not perform satisfactorily, when there is serious deterioration in the affairs of the business, or a reduction in the value of the security provided, and
- the amount of credit granted is based on the lender's assessment of the creditworthiness of the company, its principals and the credit requested, among other factors.

(c) Term loans

A term loan is generally money borrowed for a term of one year up to 10 years. The regular loan repayments include principal and interest, and are usually for a fixed aggregate amount over the life or term of the loan agreement.

Term loans are commonly used to provide funds to buy an existing business, to help finance expansions or capital expenditure, and to provide additional working capital for a growing business.

While the majority of term loans are secured by collateral such as fixed assets, or other chattels (cars, building, land, equipment), the lender places great importance upon the ability of the borrower to repay his or her indebtedness out of the business's earnings over the life of the loan.

The main characteristics of a term loan are:

- it may be repaid over a period of time generally related

to the useful 'life' of the assets; for example, car — three to five years; land and buildings — after three years,

- the lender will only give you a percentage of the value; for example, car 80 per cent; buildings 75 per cent; the other 20 or 25 per cent of the cost of the asset must come from the equity you have in the company, or new funds from shareholders or yourself,

- the company must be able to show the lender that future sales will generate enough cash to repay the loan,

- there are different lenders for different types of term loans. One consideration in the approval of your proposal is 'gearing' or 'debt to equity ratio'. This is the ratio of the money you owe, to the money you put in the business. Generally, the lender's assessment of this ratio is discretionary, but if you are a new business, or just building up a reputation, it is unlikely that the lender will want to go beyond 2:1 or even 1:1. Consequently, this may place an additional restriction on the amount that you can borrow.

- interest rate at time of signing is slightly higher than an overdraft,

- repayment period of loan is specified and agreed upon in advance, and

- it could take longer to obtain a loan approval than an overdraft.

(d) Trade credit or supplier financing
This is the form of short-term financing used most often. Trade credit financing means that a supplier will not insist on immediate payment for purchase of merchandise. Terms can be arranged between both parties as to when payment will be made — generally 30 to 90 days.

(e) Renting or leasing
Renting or leasing assets is an alternative form of financing. Leasing companies will consider arranging a lease with option to purchase on virtually any tangible asset. Renting premises, as opposed to buying a building, is also a financing alternative. Assets such as typewriters, office furniture, personal computers or word processors, cars or other vehicles can all be leased. The advantages of leasing are:

- it frees equity capital for investment in areas of greater return,

- it frees borrowing power for the more critical areas of the business,
- no down payment is required with leasing,
- rates are usually fixed for a set term,
- the full payment is an allowable expense, and
- purchase options can be exercised at a later date at a predetermined price.

There are also disadvantages. You should discuss the tax and financial considerations with your accountant before you make your decision.

Sources of financing

1. Equity

The most common source of equity capital is personal funds from savings. In exchange for the funds provided to the company, the owner obtains all the shares of the company or ownership of the business.

Equity can be further increased from the savings of friends willing to invest, from relatives, or from venture capitalists. However, small business people have often created problems by bringing in friends or relatives as investors. Conflicts can occur if the business does not do as well as everyone initially imagined, or the terms and conditions of loans are not clearly spelled out, or if the lenders or investors insist on becoming involved in day-to-day operations.

Any agreement between the parties should be documented in writing and signed in advance to eliminate any misunderstanding. Agreement should be reached on the rate of interest to be paid, when the loans will be repaid, any options you have to pay them back early, and the procedures that all parties will follow if the loans are not repaid on time. Take competent legal advice in advance to protect your interests.

An equity investment can be in the form of loans, or common stock or shares in the company, or a combination of loans and shares. The investment structure will vary in each situation.

Generally speaking, the advantage of money being invested as shareholder loans is that it can be paid back to lenders without tax, other than personal tax on interest you receive before the loan is paid off. If the money is in the form of shares, it is much more difficult to withdraw since shares must be sold to someone else, and may be subject to capital gains tax. Long-term debt investors may therefore place restrictions on when and how the company can pay off loans, redeem shares, or possibly even pay dividends on shares. These restrictions are imposed to protect the long-term debt invested.

The advice of a tax accountant is recommended since your personal tax situation and that of other potential equity investors could have a bearing on whether the shareholders' investment should be in the form of loans or share purchase. There are various factors that a potential investor will consider when assessing the attractiveness of your business proposal. Remember that a venture capital firm will be far more exacting than relatives or friends.

2. Debt

Commercial banks are a major source of capital for new and continuing small ventures. Additional organisations that provide financing include insurance companies, pension companies and merchant banks.

There is considerable competition between banks and other financial institutions. Compare at least three different financial institutions to assess the most favourable loan package available.

Remember that all aspects of financial dealings are negotiable. Obtain the lending terms in writing before you sign. Don't rush into a relationship with a financial institution without reasonably exploring all the other alternatives. In addition, have your outside advisers, such as your accountant or solicitor, review the terms. Obtain the advice of your partners.

The Business Loan Guarantee scheme is a government incentive to small businesses, administered through the banks. Your bank has to be satisfied that the business plan looks workable and, in cases where the bank is doubtful about offering finance on conventional terms, the government will guarantee the risk up to 70 per cent of the advance. The interest rate is around 2.5 per cent over base rate on the guaranteed portion of the loan.

In certain circumstances, government finance is also available through agencies such as the Scottish Development Agency, the Mid Wales Development Board and, in England, the Council for Small Industries in Rural Areas. It is first necessary to find out whether your business is eligible for government help and it may be that the Small Firms Service should be the first port of call.

Tips on approaching your lender

When you approach a financial institution, you must sell the merits of your business proposal. As in all sales presentations, consider the needs and expectations of the other party. A lender will be interested in the following:

(a) Your familiarity with the business concept and the realities of the market-place, as reflected in your detailed business plan.

(b) Your ability to service the debt with sufficient surplus to cover contingencies, including interest charges, so that you eventually repay the debt in full, as demonstrated in your cash flow forecast.

(c) Your level of commitment, as shown by your equity in the business or cash investment in the particular asset being purchased.

(d) Your secondary source of repayment, including security in the event of default, and other sources of income.

(e) Your track record and integrity, as shown in your personal credit history, your business plan and business results or past business experience.

(f) Your approach. During the loan interview remember you're doing business as though with a customer. Don't be subservient, overly familiar or too aggressive. Keep in mind that a lender is in business for the same reason that you are − to make a profit. Don't try to appeal to a lender's social conscience. It won't work; loans aren't granted for their social impact.

(g) Your judgement in supplying information. Be sensible with the number of documents you provide at the outset. You do not want to overwhelm the lender with too much material. For example, an introductory page and summary of your business plan provide a good basic loan submission if the amount requested is small. You should have all the other documents prepared and available if requested. See Chapter 12 when preparing your business plan.

(h) Your personal appearance. You should present yourself in a manner that projects self-confidence and success.

(i) Your mental alertness. What times during the day are you at your mental peak? This should be the time that you arrange for an interview with the bank manager.

(j) Your consideration in allowing sufficient lead time for approval. The lender needs a reasonable time to assess your proposal. Also, the loan may have to be reviewed by another level within the financial institution.

(k) Your credit rating.

If your request for financing is approved, find out everything you need to know about the conditions, terms, payment methods, interest rates, security requirements, and any other fees to be paid. No commitment to accept the financing should be made until all this information is provided and understood, and its impact on the proposed business analysed. Ask your accountant to assist you in the loan application in advance and review the bank's approval. Make certain you get the approval particulars in writing.

Why loans are turned down

If a request for financing is not approved, find out why. Use the lender's experience to your advantage. Lenders handle many requests for financing, and have experience in the financial aspects of many businesses, even if they do not have direct management experience.

If there is something specifically wrong with the financing proposal, see if it can be corrected and then re-apply. If not, use this knowledge when approaching other potential lenders, or on future occasions when seeking funds.

Some of the causes of a loan rejection could be the following:

(a) The business idea might be considered unsound or

too risky. A lender's judgement is generally based on past performance of other businesses similar to the one you are proposing.

(b) You may have insufficient collateral. A lender must satisfy itself that there are sufficient assets pledged to meet the outstanding debt if your business does not succeed financially. If you are just starting a business, a lender generally requires you to pledge personal assets such as your home, car and other securities against the loan. If you are borrowing funds under a corporate name, your personal guarantee will generally be requested, and in some cases your spouse's guarantee as well, depending upon the circumstances. In the lender's opinion, you may not have sufficient security required for the amount of loan you are requesting.

(c) There may be a lack of financial commitment on your part. Lenders are reluctant to approve loan financing for business ventures if borrowers are not fully committed. The lender does not want to foreclose or repossess and then have to sell assets to collect your money. The lender will therefore want to know how much personal capital you have made available to the business venture in order to assess your commitment to repay the loan. If you have not made any financial commitment and yet have security that you wish to pledge, the security alone may not be sufficient.

(d) A lender could reject your loan application if you have not prepared a detailed business plan or do not understand its significance.

(e) The purpose of the loan is not explained or is not acceptable. It is important that the specific use of the funds being borrowed be outlined in detail. It is also important that the purpose and amount of funds being requested be reasonable and appropriate. For example, it could be considered unreasonable for you to budget for a large fee or salary from your business in the first six months. If you intend to use the loan to pay off past debts or financial obligations, it may not be approved since the funds would not be directly generating cash flow for your new business venture.

(f) Your character, personality, or stability can affect a lender's decision. It is important to appear confident, enthusiastic, well informed, and realistic. If your personality is not consistent with the personality required for your type of business in the eyes of the lender, it could have a negative effect. If you are going through a separation or divorce proceedings, have declared personal bankruptcy, or had business failures in the past, these factors could have an adverse impact on your loan application.

Now that you know the factors that institutional lenders take into account when considering a loan application, evaluate your own business proposal on those criteria. Use the worksheet on page 153 to isolate any weaknesses in your proposal.

Types of security a lender may require

Lenders primarily lend money to businesses that exhibit a strong potential to repay. Nevertheless, they want to be covered in case of a default. Sometimes your signature is the only security the lender needs when making a loan. The kind and amount of security depends on the lender and on the borrower's situation. The most common types of security or collateral are discussed below.

1. Endorser

Borrowers often get other people to sign a note in order to bolster their own credit. These endorsers are contingently liable for the note they sign. If the borrower fails to pay off the loan, the lender expects the endorser to make the note good. Sometimes the endorser may be asked to pledge assets or securities as well.

2. Guarantor

A guarantor is a person who guarantees the payment of a note by signing a guarantee commitment. Lenders often require a personal guarantee from company directors as security for loans advanced to the company. If the company defaults on its obligations, the lender has a choice of suing the guarantor or the company or both for the amounts outstanding.

Loan application worksheet

Assessment factor	Poor		Good	Excellent	
	1	2	3	4	5
1. Personal credit rating	—	—	—	—	—
2. Capacity to pay back loan from business assets if business fails	—	—	—	—	—
3. Collateral to pay back loan from personal assets if business fails	—	—	—	—	—
4. Character (as perceived in the community)	—	—	—	—	—
5. Commitment (your personal investment of time, energy, and money)	—	—	—	—	—
6. Clarity and completeness of your business plan	—	—	—	—	—
7. Viability of business concept (eg moderate risk)	—	—	—	—	—
8. Past personal experience in the nature of the proposed business	—	—	—	—	—
9. Past successful experience in your own business	—	—	—	—	—
10. Balanced management team available	—	—	—	—	—
11. Suitability of your personality to the pressures and responsibilities of the business	—	—	—	—	—

What would you do to improve the weak areas where you have rated yourself 1 or 2?

_____

_____

_____

After making your assessment of the strengths and weaknesses of your loan possibilities, what negotiating strategies would you use to convince the lender?

_____

_____

_____

_____

Try to negotiate a limited guarantee to cover the shortfall in the security, if other securities have been pledged. Be very careful not to sign a personal guarantee for the full amount of the loan if at all possible. Recover your guarantee as soon as the business has paid off its obligation or can carry the debt on its own security. Resist having your spouse sign a personal guarantee of your debts. Also attempt to avoid signing personal guarantees on your corporate obligations to the landlord, leasing companies, and general creditors. Your personal guarantee is often all you have left to negotiate on a future occasion. Remember, the main purpose of using a company is to avoid personal liability. Small business people are frequently too naive and generous in giving out personal guarantees.

3. Promissory note

A promissory note is a written promise to pay a specified sum of money to the lender, either on demand or at a specified future time.

4. Demand loan

A demand loan involves a written promise to pay the amount of monies outstanding to the lender upon demand.

5. Mortgage

A lender may require a mortgage against your property for the advancement of funds. It could be a first, second or third mortgage against your property, or a collateral mortgage to a guarantee or demand note.

6. Postponement of claim

If there are any loans from shareholders, the lender may ask for an agreement that the company will not repay the shareholders until the lender has been repaid in full.

7. Pledge of stocks or bonds

The possession of stocks and bonds may be transferred to the lender, but title remains with the borrower. The security must be marketable.

The lender may ask the borrower for additional security or payment whenever the market value of the stocks or bonds drops below the lender's required margin.

8. Assignment of life assurance

A lender may request that the borrower assign the proceeds of a life assurance policy to the lender up to the amount outstanding at the time of death of the borrower. Another form of assignment is against the cash surrender value of a life assurance policy.

9. Assignment of lease or rents

The assignment of a lease is fairly common security in franchises, so that the franchisor can assume the lease if the franchisee goes out of business or defaults on the franchise agreement. The franchisor could then resell the franchise with a lease in place.

With rents, a lender may ask you to sign a document that would not be used by the bank unless you were in default of your loan obligations. In the event of your default, all rents that you had been previously collecting from tenants or subtenants would be diverted directly to the bank. The bank would notify the tenants and provide them with a copy of the assignment document.

10. Warehouse receipts

Banks lend money with commodities as security. A warehouse receipt is frequently given to the bank and shows that the merchandise used as security either has been placed in a public warehouse or has been left on your premises under the control of one of your employees, who is bonded. The bank lends a percentage of the estimated value of only the goods that are readily marketable.

11. Floor plan contracts

The only way that many small businesses can afford to have displays such as vehicles, appliances, or boats is to obtain them if the title to the merchandise is conditional on purchase. This is called a 'floor plan contract'. In other words, either the manufacturer lends the items to the retailer, or the bank lends money for purchase of the merchandise on the condition that a trust receipt is signed showing the serial-numbered merchandise. This document requires that you acknowledge receipt of the merchandise, agree to keep it in trust for the bank, and promise to pay the bank as you sell the goods.

12. Debenture

A debenture is a very powerful document to give as security, but can only be given by a corporation. It is like a floating mortgage over the corporation and all its assets — present and future. If you are in default of the loan conditions, and the bank activates the debenture, it does so by appointing a receiver. The receiver takes over the company on behalf of the bank and either sells the company or its assets to pay the bank back its loan. Occasionally you may have the ability to refinance the loan with funds from some other source, but once a receiver is appointed your financial gearing to get funds elsewhere generally is reduced for obvious reasons.

As a final reminder, be very careful when negotiating your security package. Lenders will usually ask for a lot more security than they really need for the loan. They prefer to be over-secured. Your challenge is to find a lending institution that will accept a reasonable security package for your loan. This will allow you to retain unpledged assets that you may require at some future point. For example, the more personal guarantees you sign, the more contingent personal liability you have. You therefore have less personal negotiating leverage or bargaining ability.

In summary, it is critical that you consult your solicitor and accountant before signing any security documentation. You may want to apply to another lender or renegotiate the loan. Remember, if you give all your security the first time, you have nothing left to negotiate if you require additional funds at some future point. Use the worksheet on page 157 to determine which type of financial security you are prepared to offer.

Loan security worksheet

Now that you have reviewed various types of financial security, list those that you would have available (not necessarily what you would be prepared to give).

_____

_____

_____

List the types and amount of financial security that you would be prepared to pledge if the funds you requested were approved. What factors were important in arriving at your bottom line?

_____

_____

_____

Detail the negotiating strategies you will use to convince the lender that the security package you are proposing is fair.

_____

_____

_____

More techniques for raising money *

There are many ways of obtaining money other than going to a bank or financial institution. Go through this section and check those areas you feel have potential or that you would like to explore further. Then write out why you think the source has potential, how much money might be available from that source, how long it will take to obtain the money, the personal sacrifices that you are prepared to make, and the price or security that you are prepared to pledge.

1. Personal assets

Your first source of financing would be your personal posses-

* These techniques for raising money are quoted from _Getting Money_ by Richard D Smith' © '1981 (International Self-Counsel Press Ltd, Vancouver).

sions. By cashing in or selling assets, pledging them at the bank as security for loan, re-evaluating your insurance, or using credit, a sizeable amount of money can be raised and saved. Here are some ideas:

- Refinance your home
- Sell your second car
- Sell your personal business assets to your business
- Borrow against the cash surrender value of your life assurance policy
- Use your personal savings account
- Cash in your stocks, shares, antiques, art, jewellery and coins
- Cash in your pension plans
- Cash in other savings plans (such as National Savings)
- Sell extra personal possessions
- Use short-term credit to conserve cash (credit cards or bank overdraft)
- Re-evaluate and consolidate your life assurance programme (eg convert whole life to term life).

2. Reduce your lifestyle

After you look closely at your personal or family budget you should find many ways that you can save on unnecessary expenditure. The more money you save, the more money will be available for your business. Ideas:

- Cut down on alcohol, tobacco, trips and meals out
- Reduce your travel and entertainment expenses
- Consider doing part-time work in the evenings or at weekends
- Buy a less expensive or more versatile car, and
- Turn your holidays into partial business trips.

3. Family assistance

Your family may be a source of valuable assistance. They may have time, talent and other resources that could be as essential and profitable as money itself. Ideas:

- Share a family office
- Share personnel and equipment costs
- Put your family to work for you

- Put your family to work for others, and
- Use the 'family bank' to take advantage of good relations with the manager.

4. Private investors you already know

People who know you and your potential well and have faith in you could be an excellent source of funds, especially if you can demonstrate to them in a well prepared business plan that your idea is viable and justifies supporting. Ideas:

- your immediate family
- other relatives
- friends
- neighbours
- co-workers
- business associates, and
- your previous bosses.

5. Private investors new to you

There are many private individuals who would be interested in investing in a small business with a reasonable risk and solid profit potential. Again your idea, your business plan, and your presentation are the key selling points. Ideas:

- newspaper advertising
- word-of-mouth (to your stockbroker, accountant, solicitor, bank manager), and
- services for equity (professionals provide services for share ownership).

6. Professional people

Professional people have high incomes and the desire to find tax deductions, but they are frequently too busy to spend the time to find out about them. If a well researched and prepared business concept is presented, they could be a good source for small business investments. Ideas:

- your solicitor
- your accountant
- your doctor
- your dentist
- your estate agent

- your personal or commercial insurance agent, and
- other good salespeople you know.

7. Your customers

Your customers are already prepared to pay their money for your product, service, or idea. Try to get cash in hand using these techniques:

- deposits with all orders (eg 10 to 20 per cent or more)
- discounts for prepayments (eg 2 per cent net 10 days)
- credit card orders
- mail order on a cash-with-order basis
- charges against the customer's credit card or phone number (eg for business-related expenses)
- progress invoicing (eg invoice every week rather than 30 days).

8. Your suppliers

Suppliers can assist your venture with credit (which is as useful as cash), or by letting you make partial or late payments for goods. There are various ways suppliers can finance you:

- Order goods on consignment (ie do not pay the supplier until the customer pays you).
- Secure trade credit (you might obtain credit for 30, 60 or 90 days).
- Secure extended payment terms.
- Schedule partial payments.
- Don't prepay suppliers (eg remit supplier funds when goods are ready for despatch, not in advance).

9. Employees as investors

If employees can see the value in your product or service, you can offer them various incentives to obtain their money in return for their obtaining a return on their investment. There could also be additional benefits to you in terms of increased productivity, higher profitability, and lower absenteeism. Ideas:

- cash investments
- bonus based on employee investment
- deferred profit-sharing plans

- stock option plans, and
- a bonus based on increased productivity or cost cuts.

10. Government agencies

When dealing with government sources it is important to keep in mind that you will often need formal documentation. Check with the funding sources first, so that your financial proposal can be adapted to their information needs. For example, you might be required to provide detailed documentation on your personal and business cash position; your company's eligibility for the grant, subsidy, or loan; your projections for sales or other measurable forms of success; and the qualifications, credentials and expertise of you and your management team.

Some forms of government finance have been mentioned on pages 148-9 but others might also apply:

Enterprise Allowance Scheme
Under this, an allowance of £40 per week can be paid for one year to someone who has been registered unemployed for eight weeks or more and can show a viable plan for self-employment. One condition is that the person must have £1000 available to invest in the project. Details are obtainable from Department of Employment offices, Jobcentres etc.

Business Expansion Scheme
This is likely to be of interest if loans between £25,000 and £250,000 are sought. The scheme is administered by venture capital companies who have special investment arrangements to raise funds. Certain companies are excluded from participation, for example those in the financial sector, property dealers, farming, firms involved in dealing other than in normal retail or wholesale distribution. Firms whose shares are quoted on the Stock Exchange or the Unlisted Securities Market are also excluded from borrowing through the scheme.

11. Sell ownership

To get your business started or to help it through difficult times, you may wish to consider selling part of your equity to keep solvent or to obtain capital without going into debt. Ideas:

- Take on active or sleeping partners, and
- Incorporate and sell shares.

12. Leasing

Leasing is an effective way to reduce your cash outlay, leaving you with more money to use in generating sales or profits. Almost anything can be leased. For a monthly fee, you obtain the use of the goods, services, or equipment, while the owner is responsible for maintenance, servicing, insurance, and other costs. Ideas:

- Lease assets and equipment instead of buying
- Lease your own assets back to yourself through a financier, and
- Rent space from another tenant.

13. Renting

Another way to save money on offices, equipment, and skilled personnel is through temporary service organizations. This can permit you to make short-term financial commitments for equipment and services you will require for only a few weeks or months. Ideas:

- Rent office equipment and furnishings, and
- Rent office services (eg secretarial, telephone answering, word processing, postal address).

14. Other sources

Here are additional sources to approach for money, as well as creative techniques for saving money:

- pension funds
- family investment corporations or estates
- mortgage brokers
- foundations — charitable, fraternal and religious
- small business development agencies or small business investment companies
- factoring companies
- assignment of exclusive rights, patents, copyrights
- licensing
- bartering or contra accounts.

Chapter 10

Insurance

Proper risk management means planning for potential problems and attempting to insure against them. You should be familiar with the numerous types of insurance available, the method of obtaining the insurance, the best way to reduce premiums, and the pitfalls to avoid.

Obtaining insurance

Insurance companies market their services chiefly through the methods discussed below.

1. Agents

Agents are self-employed, and place life, home, car, or other common types of insurance with the insurance companies with which they have formal links. In some cases, agents are under an obligation to place a certain volume of insurance with each company they deal with in order to earn their commission. Therefore, it is possible that you might be sold policies that may not suit your needs. You may get excellent advice, but based on a restricted choice.

2. Insurance brokers

Insurance brokers must be registered to describe themselves legally as 'brokers'. They claim to have complete independence from any insurance company. Generally, brokers from the larger companies are more knowledgeable and flexible in the types of coverage and policies available, and they specialise in certain areas. A broker *should* have no vested interest in placing insurance with any particular company, but as they earn their income from commission, the rate of which may vary between insurance companies, one cannot expect total impartiality. A good one will attempt to get you the best price and the best coverage to meet your needs.

Banks may also offer insurance; treat their advice with the same caution you would apply to any other source.

As in all matters of obtaining professional advice or assistance, you should have a minimum of three competitive quotes, and an opportunity to evaluate the relative strengths and weaknesses of each. If the brokers are using the same insurance base for the best coverage and premiums, then all three brokers should recommend, in theory, the same insurance companies for the different forms of coverage that you are requesting.

3. Trade associations

Ask your trade association or chamber of commerce about group rates for insurance or special trade packages. These organisations frequently have various types of insurance coverage available at a reduced group rate.

Planning your insurance

It is important to consider all criteria to determine the best type of insurance for you and your business. Your goal should be adequate coverage. That can be achieved by a periodic review of risk, and by keeping your agent informed of any changes in your business that could potentially affect your coverage.

The following principles will help you plan an insurance programme:

(a) Identify the risk to which your business is exposed.
(b) Cover your largest risk first.
(c) Determine the magnitude of loss that the business can bear without financial difficulty, and spend your money where the protection need is greatest.
(d) Decide what kind of protection will work best for each risk:
  ● absorbing risks
  ● minimising risks

- insuring against risks with commercial insurance.
(e) Insure the correct risk.
(f) Use every means possible to reduce the cost of insurance:
    - Negotiate for lower premiums if loss experience is low.
    - Shop around for comparable rates and analyse insurance terms and provisions offered by different insurance companies.
(g) Risk exposure changes, so a periodic review will save you from insuring matters that are no longer exposed to the same degree of risk. Conversely, you may need to increase limits of liability. Reviews can help to avoid overlaps and gaps in coverage, and thereby keep your risk and premiums lower.
(h) If you are pleased with the way a particular broker handles your various forms of insurance, it is preferable to be selective and use just that one broker. An advantage of the large brokerage firms is that they have a pool of insurance experts who can help you in various areas of the business.
(i) Attempt to keep your losses down in every way. Although your business may have adequate coverage, losses could be uninsurable or exempt from cover. Problems with insurance coverage could seriously affect the survival of your business.

Types of business and personal insurance

The types of insurance you might need will vary depending on the type of business you have. The following overview of insurance policies is provided to make you aware of what exists, and what might be appropriate in your situation.

These descriptions are not recommendations; only you can decide on an insurance policy after an objective assessment of your needs following comparative research in a competitive insurance market.

1. General liability insurance

Employer's liability and public liability insurance are compulsory in law. Employers are legally liable for bodily injuries to employees which arise out of, or in the course of, employment. Businesses are responsible for injuries to members of the public which arise from a lack of care. The user of a vehicle must insure to cover bodily injury to third parties and the cost of emergency treatment following an accident in which his vehicle is involved.

Obligatory forms of insurance apply also to specific trades or professions, such as riding establishments, solicitors, insurance brokers, operators of nuclear installations and merchant vessel owners. In all these cases, insurance is required to safeguard the interests of innocent third parties.

A general liability policy covers negligence causing injury to clients, employees, and the general public. The policy is normally written up as a comprehensive liability policy. Trade organisations will sometimes offer a package to members which includes their specific requirements.

Other insurances will be dictated by common prudence:

2. Product liability insurance

This policy offers protection against a lawsuit by a customer or client who used your product or service and, as a result, sustained bodily injury or property damage from it.

3. Professional indemnity

This coverage protects you against litigation arising from loss or injury incurred by your clients as a result of a lack of skill and/or judgement in your dealings with them.

4. Motor vehicle liability insurance

This coverage includes other people's property, other vehicles, persons in other vehicles, and persons in the insured vehicle. If you are using your car for business purposes, exclusively or occasionally, it is important that your premium should cover business use. It is possible that your current motor vehicle insurance policy has a premium based on personal use only. Problems could occur if there were an accident and it was discovered that your car was indeed used for business purposes.

5. Fire and theft insurance

You probably already have fire and theft insurance if you are working from home. You should make sure your home business use would not allow the insurance company to deny your claim. If you are working in an office or commercial premises, it is important to make sure that you have satisfactory coverage.

6. Business interruption insurance

The indirect loss from fire or theft can be greater than the loss itself. If your premises or files are destroyed, you can lose revenue. Certain expenses must still be met. Such a situation could put a severe strain on working capital, and seriously affect the survival of the business. Business interruption insurance is designed to cover the period between the time of the loss and the return to normal operating conditions. The insurance policy could also include the costs of temporarily renting other premises.

7. Insurance for legal expenses

This cover could be taken out by businesses exposed to the risks of legal actions arising from a variety of legislation. It may be considered that the legal costs would outweigh the value of any award and further insurance is a prudent investment.

8. Money insurance

Such a policy would cover you for the loss of money in all its forms, for example: cash, bank notes, cheques, postal orders, money orders, postage stamps and luncheon vouchers. Cover can be provided for loss from the premises, in transit, or from any other insured premises.

9. Glass insurance

Glass is usually covered under a combined shop policy but some firms are more at risk than others and would need special cover, for example supermarkets.

10. Fidelity guarantee

This provides cover in the event of theft by employees who handle cash or stock. The insurer will probably insist that a defaulter is prosecuted.

11. Personal accident and sickness assurance

You could possibly be disabled for a short or long period of time. This insurance pays you a certain monthly amount if you are permanently disabled or sick, or a portion of that amount if you are partially disabled, but capable of generating some income.

12. Key-person insurance

The death or disability of a key person could seriously affect the earning power of your business. For example, if you have an associate, or partner who is critical to a particularly large project or your business as a whole, key-person insurance should be considered.

The loss of a key person may decrease the confidence of your existing or potential clients or customers which, in turn, could lead to a loss of future contracts, competitive position, and revenue, and the expense of finding and training a replacement. The amount and type of key-person insurance will depend upon many factors, as designing an evaluation formula for a key person is difficult.

13. Shareholders' or partners' insurance

If it is your intention to have a partner in your business or a shareholder in your company, you may wish to consider shareholder or partnership insurance. Normally this type of insurance is part of a buy-sell agreement that allows for a deceased shareholder's or partner's interest to be purchased by the surviving partners or shareholders of the company. It can also be used to buy out the share in the business of a retiring partner.

In the absence of a buy-sell agreement funded by life assurance, the death of a partner could cause the immediate dissolution of the partnership. Unless there is an express agreement to the contrary, the surviving partner's duty is to liquidate the business, collect all outstanding accounts, pay off all debts, and account as trustee to the personal representative of the deceased partner for the value of the deceased's interest in the business.

In the case of a company, the deceased shareholder's interest would be considered an asset and would go to the beneficiary named in the will, if one existed. Naturally, the introduction of a new shareholder who owns an interest in the company, especially a majority interest, could have an unsettling effect on the shareholders and the company's continued operation.

In summary, the procedure is that each partner or shareholder applies for a life assurance policy on the life of the other. The applicant is the beneficiary and pays the premiums on his or her partner's life assurance policy. When a partner dies, the funds from the insurance are received by the beneficiary (the partner). These funds are then used to purchase the deceased partner's share of the business. The surviving partner retains control of the business, and the heirs of the deceased get cash for their interest.

14. Term assurance

This type of insurance insures a life for a specific period of time, then terminates. The most common minimum period is five years. If the insured dies within the term of the policy, the insurance company pays the full face amount to the heirs. The cost of premiums is based on life expectancy for the person's age during the five-year period. Term assurance does not have a cash or loan value.

Because term assurance can be written for various periods, and the premiums are inexpensive, it is valuable to the business person. There is generally a reduced rate for non-smokers. Such term policies are often used to provide collateral security for loans to the firm or for personal obligations.

It is highly advisable to have term assurance for at least the amount of your personal financial obligations, and business financial obligations for which you have a direct or contingent liability. This is an area that is frequently overlooked.

15. Medical insurance

It is important to take out sufficient medical coverage for your needs. If you are doing any business outside the country, you should have extended coverage that pays for any medical bills that may be incurred by injury or illness while you are abroad.

Types of insurance	Required (Yes/No)	Annual cost	Payment schedule
1. General liability insurance			
2. Product liability insurance			
3. Professional indemnity insurance			
4. Motor vehicle liability insurance			
5. Fire and theft insurance			
6. Business interruption insurance			
7. Insurance for legal expenses			
8. Money insurance			
9. Glass insurance			
10. Fidelity guarantee			
11. Personal accident and sickness insurance			
12. Key-person insurance			
13. Shareholders' or partners' insurance			
14. Term assurance			
15. Medical insurance			
16. Group insurance			
Total annual cost		£	

Figure 9.
Insurance planning checklist

16. Group insurance

You may be eligible for group insurance rates if you have four or more employees. The policies of insurance companies vary, but medical and dental plans are available for small groups.

After you have considered your various insurance needs, fill in the insurance planning checklist outlined in Figure 9.

Chapter 11

Credit Control, Invoicing and Collection

Many people starting out in business are unsophisticated when it comes to developing a clear credit control and invoicing policy. In many cases the prospective entrepreneur has had no previous business experience and does not realise the pitfalls that can occur.

A consistent system is essential to your survival. It does not take many bad debts to eliminate the profit of your business for the whole year. In more serious cases, you could go out of business if substantial debts owed by clients or customers are not paid.

A number of common mistakes occur when people begin a business. First, they want to build up a clientele and reputation as quickly as possible by extending credit to too many customers without proper checks and balances. Second, the new entrepreneur may be too busy or too inexperienced to monitor debtors carefully. Third, unpaid bills are not followed up quickly with appropriate steps to collect funds. The effect of this sloppy approach can be fatal to your business.

This chapter outlines the pitfalls to be aware of and the procedures to adopt when reviewing your credit control policy. If you develop the correct system for your needs, it will enhance your cash flow and profit, and minimise stress, customer problems, and bad debts.

Disadvantages of extending credit

When you extend credit, the understanding is that the customer intends to pay, is capable of paying, and that nothing will occur to prevent the client from paying. You assume that most customers are honest and acting in good faith. Many of these assumptions may not be accurate.

There are a number of potential disadvantages to extending credit. First, extending credit may take a great deal of your time and the administrative paperwork, checking references, and monitoring and following up on slow paying clients may be tedious. Second, the expense of credit checking and collection could be more than you are able to pay. Expenses could consist of credit reference fees, collection costs, legal fees, and time lost that you could otherwise spend generating revenue. Finally, you may need to increase your working capital requirements to keep your business in operation because of unpaid debts. You will be paying interest on the additional money you may have to borrow to offset your decreased working capital.

Assessing the customer

It is important to be very careful when extending credit. Apply the following general guidelines to your business.

(a) Develop a clear credit policy for your business after consultation with your accountant. Experienced professional advice is essential before you extend credit. Some of the factors that will influence your company's credit policy include:
- nature and size of business
- overall business objectives
- general policy of the business
- product or service requirements
- channels of distribution
- conditions of competition
- socio-economic classes of customers
- price of the product or service
- expectations of customer, and
- nature of credit in your type of industry.

(b) Develop a credit application that has all the necessary information for your files.

(c) Consider using a credit reporting agency such as Dun & Bradstreet. Obtain and review industry and trade association reports for your type of business. Check into the past debt payment profile of your potential client in advance.

(d) Obtain and check references from your client if appropriate. Ask about the client's length of time in business.

(e) Carefully consider the amount of credit being extended. The greater the amount of money unpaid, the greater the risk for you.

(f) If the business you have is highly specialised, and you have very little competition, then you have a lot of leverage in the nature of credit that you would be extending.

(g) If the customer is a large institution or government department, ask about the customary length of time for accounts rendered to be paid. Specify in your contract the exact terms of payment. Payments from such customers can be delayed for months by bureaucracy or a simple reluctance to pay up.

(h) If the customer requests deferred payments, you run the risk of default or other problems. Sometimes customers request a deferred payment. If you are faced with a decision about deferred payment, you should consider charging interest on the total amount, charging higher prices, requesting a sizeable down payment before you release the goods (to cover your cost), or obtaining collateral to protect yourself if the costs are substantial.

(i) Consider the future benefit of a relationship with the prospective customer. If there is a realistic possibility of future orders or services, you may wish to weigh the potential benefits against the risks.

Minimising the risk of bad debts

There are several effective techniques to minimise the risk of bad debts. Non-paying customers may seriously affect the viability of your business. The following general guidelines may not all be appropriate for all customer/client situations; your judgement in each case must dictate the best approach.

1. Credit card payments

You may wish to consider accepting major credit cards as

payment for goods and services. You will pay a service charge that normally varies between 2½ and 5 per cent, depending on the volume of sales. In the case of Visa and Access, you can deposit the merchant slips the same day at a local bank as if they were cash. In the case of American Express and Diners Club, you have to send for the merchant payment by mail, which normally involves a one-week turnaround before you receive a cheque.

2. Special cheque clearance

For a fee, cheques can be given fast clearance through the bank. This is a useful service when you have doubts about a customer's status, or simply need to improve your cash flow quickly.

3. Advance deposit

A customer can be asked to pay a retainer or deposit of 10 to 25 per cent or more of the total contract amount prior to the service being performed or goods being ordered.

4. Prepaid disbursements

If you are providing a service that involves out-of-pocket expenses, you may wish to request prepaid disbursements. You do not want to carry your client for out-of-pocket expenses at the risk of your own cash flow. You also do not want to risk non-payment or a dispute of the overall account.

5. Progress payments

It is common for people in the service industry to request funds by means of invoicing at specific points in the project. The stages at which progress payments are to be paid would be outlined in an initial contract.

6. Regular invoicing

Statements can be sent out on a weekly or monthly basis, depending on the circumstances. It is important to outline in the contract, if appropriate, your policy on the timing of reminders. That way the customer will not be taken by surprise. This also provides you with the advantage of knowing at an early stage in the relationship if the customer is going to

175

dispute your accounts, and at that point you can either resolve the problem or discontinue your services. It can be very risky to allow substantial work to be performed or goods to be delivered before rendering an account.

7. Invoicing on time

It is important to send your invoice as soon as the goods are released, or as soon as you have provided the service.

8. Accelerated invoicing

If you sense that the customer may have problems paying the bill or other factors cause you concern, accelerate your normal invoicing pattern. You want to receive payment on your account before difficulties occur.

The risk of rendering an account that states 'net 30 days' is that the customer is not legally overdue in payment to you until after 30 days. If you become aware of customer financial problems, it is difficult to commence legal action or garnishee before the 30-day period has expired. Depending on the nature of the trade of your business, you may decide to have 'net 10 days' or 'net due upon receipt' on your invoices.

9. Withholding vital information

If you are in the service industry, and have documents, records, reports, and other material related to a customer, you may feel it appropriate, if circumstances warrant, to withhold returning all the necessary material to the customer until your account has been paid, or other appropriate arrangements made.

10. Withholding service

If customer problems occur, you may wish to stop providing your services at a critical stage until the matter has been resolved to your satisfaction. To protect yourself in this event, you should have this option spelled out in your initial contract. Also obtain legal advice for the proper protection in advance.

11. Personal guarantee of principals of a limited company

Depending on the customer, you may want to have the

principals sign a formal contract as personal guarantors. Another variation is to have the contract in the name of the company and its principals as co-covenanters of the contract. Limited companies are a potential high risk. A personal guarantee as a condition of credit is recommended, therefore, unless the customer is clearly creditworthy. Discuss this aspect with your accountant or solicitor and have him or her draw up a standard credit application with a personal guarantee provision for corporate credit.

12. Monitor payment trends of customers

Record and monitor the payment patterns of customers so you are aware of trends that could place your accounts at risk. If you see an invoice is more than a week or 10 days overdue, begin the various steps of your collection system immediately.

13. Involving customer in assignment

If you are in a service industry, try to involve the customer in some fashion during the performance of the service. By making your client aware of your services, benefits, time, and skill, you should minimise problems that could occur because of a remote relationship.

To summarise, a primary cause of bad debt loss is a credit decision based on an inadequate credit investigation. However, prompt despatch of orders or provision of services is essential; your credit checking method should be geared for speed and efficiency to enhance your potential profit.

The extent to which you investigate each customer's credit will vary with each case. You will want to consider the following:

(a) The size of the order and the potential for future orders
(b) The status of the present account
(c) The length of time the customer has been in business
(d) The amount of time until delivery or provision of service
(e) Whether the present product is seasonal and how it relates to the products offered by the competition
(f) The relationship of the order to the total credit

exposure of the customer

(g) Whether the customer is a limited company, partnership, or sole trader

(h) Whether the credit risk falls within the firm's credit policy

(i) If it is a special order, whether a deposit is required, or if delivery is on a COD basis.

Collecting late payments without legal action

If you have established appropriate precautionary measures and a solid credit and invoicing policy, you should have very few overdue accounts. However, in any business, late payments will occur for several different reasons:

(a) The customer is indifferent to your deadlines.

(b) The customer has a sloppy attitude about paying accounts and is accustomed to being pressured or reminded before paying.

(c) Institutional or government payment procedures sometimes involve a long wait for payment.

(d) A customer may deliberately delay payment in order to save money at your expense. You save the customer interest on working capital if he or she can use your money for free. You should have an interest factor for overdue accounts built into your initial contract, which should act as an incentive for the customer to pay on time. A statement with the interest factor noted on it is not, in itself, evidence of an agreement between the parties. Sign a contract.

(e) A customer may prefer to give priority to other creditors where pressure to pay is greater.

(f) The customer may not have the money. This does not mean, necessarily, that the customer is going out of business, but may have a cash flow problem at that particular time.

Because of the expense, time wasted, stress, and uncertainty of legal action, it is preferable to collect as much as you can from customers yourself. Some steps that you may wish to consider are as follows:

(a) Send out a reminder invoice with a courteous comment

that the invoice is overdue. Alternatively, telephone the bought ledger department or the customer directly to ask when the payment can be expected. Courteously ask if there was possibly a misunderstanding, or if they need further information or clarification on any matter. Make sure that you note in the customer file the date and time of the call, the person you spoke with, a summary of the conversation, and when payment can be expected.

(b) If you have not received payment within a week of the preceding step, send a letter outlining that the account is in arrears and that it is to be paid under the terms of the contract. The other alternative is to telephone the customer again and ask about the reason for the delay.

(c) Another technique is to ask when the cheque will be ready. Say that you will be around to pick up the cheque or will arrange for a courier service to pick it up as soon as they telephone your office to advise that it is ready.

(d) If the customer has still not paid after you try the preceding steps, discontinue further services or supply of goods.

(e) If the customer is unable to pay because of cash flow problems or other financial difficulties, you have to assess your options. If the customer is not disputing the bill and wishes to have credit, then you have three options:

- *Instalment payment plan.* The customer agrees to pay portions on specific dates and sends you the amounts owing upon receipt of statements from you. Interest charges are negotiable.

- *Post-dated cheques.* You receive post-dated cheques from the customer over the agreed period, and in the agreed amount. You and your customer negotiate interest charges.

- *Promissory note.* The customer signs a promissory note agreeing to the total amount of the debt and the date on which the debt would be paid. The note should be signed by the principals if the customer is a limited company. Interest on the full amount of the debt should be built into the promissory note.

Legal action

If it is apparent that the customer has no intention of paying you, is objecting to your bill, or is unable to pay you, then legal action must be considered. At this stage, you are not interested in keeping the customer for present or future business; you just want to salvage the best of a bad situation. There are basically three legal options available.

1. Debt collectors

You may wish to assign the debt to a collection agency for which you will be charged between 25 and 50 per cent of the amount collected, which is better than writing the account off as a total loss. Different agencies have different styles of collection, and one agency may achieve better results with your bad debts than another. If your customer pays you directly during the period of the contract with the collection agency, you are normally obliged to pay the commission to the collection agency. Collection agencies are listed in the Yellow Pages under Debt Collectors.

2. County court

The county court is a relatively quick, informal, and inexpensive method of taking your customer to court for a small claim. However, even if you are successful and obtain a judgment against your customer, you are not guaranteed payment. There are additional steps that you will have to take, such as garnisheeing the customer or filing a judgment against the title of any properties owned by your customer.

3. Other legal action

Solicitors can be very effective in the collection of debts if you act promptly and select one who is experienced in the law and tactics of collecting. Solicitors generally charge on an hourly basis, and the more time spent trying to collect a debt, the more money it will cost you without any assurance that you will be successful in court. Even if you are successful in court and do obtain a judgment, your customer could be bankrupt or judgment proof in terms of assets, so you will never be paid. The litigation process can be protracted,

Credit policy worksheet

1. Do you intend to grant credit in your business? If so, why? If not, why not?

   _____

   _____

   _____

2. What techniques for minimising bad debts are appropriate in your business? List them, and outline why you believe they will be effective.

   _____

   _____

   _____

   _____

3. If you decide to extend credit, will you be the credit controller or will someone else look after this? List seven qualities that you believe are particularly important for an effective credit controller.

   (a) _____

   (b) _____

   (c) _____

   (d) _____

   (e) _____

   (f) _____

   (g) _____

uncertain, stressful, and expensive. Also, it is common for customers to counterclaim against you alleging various deficiencies on your part in an attempt to encourage a negotiated settlement or deflect your claim.

Bad debts and taxes

Keep an accurate record of any bad debt accounts and the procedures you went through to attempt to collect. Set aside a sum in your accounts to cover such losses.

Summary

The decision to offer your customers credit is one that is critical to the success of your business. Now that you have read this chapter, complete the worksheet on page 181 to help you focus on your credit policy.

Chapter 12

Preparing Your Business Plan

Planning and good management skills are vital to business success. Knowledge is power, and knowing the way to attain your goals has a powerful effect on business success. Those who do not plan have a very high probability of failure. If you do not know where you are going in your personal or business life, there is little prospect that you will arrive. A business plan is a written summary of what you hope to accomplish by being in business, and how you intend to organise your resources to meet your goals. It is an essential guide for operating your business successfully and measuring progress along the way.

The following are general guidelines only. You can obtain further financial forecasting and other business forms, booklets and information free or at a nominal cost from high street banks, and various government and commercial sources.

Why prepare a plan?

A business plan has several distinct advantages:

(a) By forcing you to think ahead and visualise, it encourages realism instead of over-optimism.

(b) It helps you to identify your customers, market area, pricing strategy and the competitive conditions under which you must operate to succeed. This process often leads to the discovery of a competitive advantage for new opportunities as well as deficiencies in your plan.

(c) Planning leads to a better competitive position relative to other similar businesses.

(d) By committing your plans to paper before you begin, your overall ability to manage the business will improve. You will be able to concentrate your efforts on the deviations from the plan before conditions become critical. You will also have time to look ahead and avoid problems before they arise.

(e) Having clear goals and a well written plan will aid decision-making and choice. You can always change your goals, but at least with a business plan you have some basis and a standard comparison to use in evaluating alternatives that may be presented to you.

(f) A business plan establishes the amount of financing or outside investment required, and when it is needed.

(g) It is very effective as a sales tool. A well organised plan makes it much easier for the lender or investor to assess your financial proposal and to assess you as a business manager. It inspires confidence in lenders and in yourself to know every aspect of the business when you are negotiating your financing. If you have a realistic, comprehensive and well documented plan, this will assist you greatly in convincing a lender.

(h) Having well established objectives helps you analyse your progress. If you have not attained your objectives by the planned time, you can make adjustments at an early stage.

(i) Three or four hours spent updating your plan each month will save considerable time and money in the long run, and may even save your business. It is essential to develop a habit of planning and reassessing on an ongoing basis.

Recommended format

The format for the business plan shown in Figure 10 is a starting point for organising your own plan. The comments following the subheadings should help you decide which sections are relevant to your business.

The business plan format normally consists of four parts: the introduction, the business concept, the financial plan, and the appendix.

The plan starts with an introductory page and summary of the highlights of the business plan. Even though your entire business is described later, a crisp one- or two-page introduction helps to capture the immediate attention of the potential investor or lender.

The business concept, which begins with a description of the industry, identifies your market potential within your industry and outlines your action plan for the coming year. Make sure your stated business goals are compatible with your personal goals, financial goals, management ability, and family considerations. The heart of the business concept is your monthly sales forecast for the coming year. As your statement of confidence in your marketing strategy, it forms the basis for your cash flow forecast and projected income statement. This section also contains an assessment of business risks and a contingency plan. Being honest about your business risks and how you plan to deal with them is the evidence of sound management.

The financial plan outlines the level of present financing and identifies the financing sought. This section should be concise. The financial plan contains projected financial forecasts, based on current information and assumptions. In carrying out your plan of action for the coming year, these operating forecasts are an essential guide to the survival and profitability of your business. It is important to refer to them often and, if circumstances dictate, rework them. Figures 11 to 14 will help you prepare a financial plan for your business.

The appendix contains all the items that do not naturally fall elsewhere in the document, or which expand further on the summaries in the document.

Estimate of start-up funds required

1. Assessment of personal monthly financial needs

Personal expenses will continue in spite of the business, and therefore have to be taken into account when determining monthly cash flow needs. It is important to calculate personal expenses accurately so that appropriate decisions can be made in terms of funding and the nature of the start-up business — whether it should start on a part-time or full-time basis, using the home as an office, or renting an outside office. (See Figure 15.)

Figure 10. *Business plan format outline*

1. *Introductory page*
   (a) Name of business
      — include address and telephone number
   (b) Legal structure
   (c) Date of start-up (or incorporation, for a limited company)
   (d) Brief details of yourself and partners (if any) or management team
      — owner's name and telephone number
   (e) Description of company
      — products or services offered by business and market area
   (f) Securities offered to investors or lenders
      — outline securities such as preferred shares, ordinary shares, debentures etc
   (g) Business loans sought
      — such as term loan, operating line of credit, mortgage
   (h) Summary of proposed use of funds

2. *Summary*
   (a) Highlights of business plan
      — preferably one-page maximum
      — include your project, competitive advantage and bottom line

3. *Table of contents*
   (a) Section titles and page numbers should be given for easy reference

4. *Description of the industry*
   (a) Industry outlook and growth potential
      — outline industry trends — past, present and future — and new developments
      — state your sources of information
   (b) Markets and customers
      — estimated size of total market, share and sales, new requirements and market trends
   (c) Competitive companies
      — market share, strengths and weaknesses, profitability, trends
   (d) National and economic trends
      — population shifts, consumer trends, relevant economic indicators

5. *Description of business venture*
   (a) Nature of business
      — characteristics, method of operation, whether performed locally, regionally, nationally or internationally

Figure 10. *Continued*

(b) Target market
—   typical clients identified by groups, present business patterns and average earnings, wants, and needs
(c) Competitive advantage of your business concept
—   your market niche, uniqueness, estimated market share
(d) Business location and size
—   location relative to market, size of premises, home or office use
(e) Staff and equipment needed
—   overall requirement, capacity, home or office use, part- or full-time staff or as required
(f) Brief history
—   principals involved in the business or proposed business, development work done, cvs and background experience of principals, cvs of key associates, if applicable

6. *Business goals*
(a) One year
—   specific goals, such as gross sales, profit margin, share of market, opening new office, introducing new service etc
(b) Over the longer term
—   return on investment, business net worth, sale of business

7. *Marketing plan*
(a) Sales strategy
—   commission sales staff, agents, employees
—   sales objectives, sales tools, sales support
—   target clients
(b) Sales approach
—   style of operation and techniques
(c) Pricing
—   costing, mark-ups, margins, break-even
(d) Promotion
—   media advertising, promotions, publicity appropriate to each target market
—   techniques of developing exposure, credibility and contacts
(e) Service policies
—   policies that your business will adopt with regard to credit and collection, tendering, types of customers
(f) Guarantees
—   service performance guarantees or other assurances will vary depending upon nature of your business and type of contract or client

Figure 10. *Continued*

   (g) Tracking methods
       — method for confirming who your clients are and how they heard about you

8. *Sales forecast*
   (a) Assumptions
       — one never has all the necessary information, so state all the assumptions made in developing the forecast
   (b) Monthly forecast for coming year
       — sales volume, projected in cash terms
   (c) Annual forecast for following two to four years
       — sales volume, projected in cash terms

The sales forecast is the starting point for your projected income statement and cash flow forecast.

9. *Production plan (manufacturing)*
   (a) Brief description of production process
       — don't be too technical
   (b) Physical plant requirements
       — building, utility requirements, expansion capability, layout
   (c) Machinery and equipment
       — new or used, lease or purchase, capacity
   (d) Raw materials
       — readily available, quality, sources
   (e) Stock requirements
       — seasonal levels, turnover rates, method of control
   (f) Suppliers
       — volume discounts, multiple sources
   (g) Personnel required
       — full-time, part-time, skill level, availability, training required
   (h) Cost of facilities, equipment and materials
       — estimates and quotations
   (i) Capital estimates
       — one time start-up or expansion capital required

10. *Operations*
   (a) Purchasing plans
       — volume discounts, multiple sources, quality, price
   (b) Inventory system
       — seasonal variation, turnover rate, method of control

Figure 10. *Continued*

    (c) Space required
       — floor and office space, improvements required, expansion capability
    (d) Staff and equipment required
       — personnel by skill level
       — fixtures, office equipment
    (e) Operations strategy

11. *Corporate structure*
    (a) Legal form
       — sole proprietorship, partnership, incorporation or cooperative
    (b) Share distribution
       — list of principal shareholders
    (c) Contracts and agreements
       — list of contracts and agreements in force
       — management contract, shareholder or partnership agreement, service contract, leases
    (d) Directors and officers
       — names and addresses, role in company
    (e) Background of management team
       — brief cvs of active owners and key employees
    (f) Supporting professional assistance
       — professionals on contract in specialised or deficient areas
    (g) Organisational chart
       — identify reporting relationships
    (h) Duties and responsibilities of key personnel
       — brief job descriptions — who is responsible for what

12. *Research and development programme*
    (a) Product or service improvements, process improvements, costs and risks

13. *Risk assessment*
    (a) Competitors' reaction
       — will competitor try to squeeze you out? What form do you anticipate any reaction will take?
    (b) List of critical external factors that might occur
       — identify effects of strikes, recession, new technology, weather, new competition, supplier problems, shifts in consumer demand, costs of delays and overruns, unfavourable industry trends

---

Figure 10. *Continued*

(c) List of critical internal factors that might occur
- income projections not realised, client dispute or litigation, credit control difficulties, demand for services increases very quickly, key employee leaves or partner becomes sick or dies

(d) Dealing with risks
- contingency plan to handle the most significant risks

14. *Overall schedule*
   (a) Interrelationship and timing of all major events important to starting and developing your business

15. *Action plan*
   (a) Steps to accomplish this year's goals
   - flow chart by month or by quarter of specific action to be taken and by whom
   (b) Checkpoint for measuring results
   - identify significant dates, sales levels as decision points

16. *Financial forecast*
   If a business has been in operation for a period of time, the previous years' balance sheets and income statements are required, preferably for the past two or three years.
   (a) Opening balance sheet
   - The balance sheet is a position statement, not an historical record; it shows what is owned and owed at a given date. There are three sections to a balance sheet: assets, liabilities, and owner's equity. You determine your firm's net worth by subtracting the liabilities from the assets.
   - Your balance sheet will indicate how your investment has grown over a period of time. Investors and lenders typically examine balance sheets to determine if the company is within acceptable assets to liability limits.
   - see Figure 11
   (b) Income and expense forecast statement (profit and loss)
   - The income and expense forecast can be described as the operating statement you would expect to see for your business at the end of the period for which the forecast is being prepared.
   - For a new business, the forecast would show what revenue and expenses you expect the business to have in its first year of operation

Figure 10. *Continued*

- It is very useful, of course, to prepare a forecast for a period longer than one year. It is suggested that a detailed operating forecast be prepared for the next year of operation and a less detailed forecast for the following two years.
- Preparing an income and expense forecast for a new business is more difficult than preparing one for an existing business, simply because in a new business there is no historical record to go by. For this reason the preparation of this forecast is an even more essential, interesting and rewarding experience than doing it for an existing business, despite the time and effort required. This analysis exercise will answer the question of whether or not a profit will be made.
- The income statement is the most difficult because it is the most uncertain at the commencement of business. It is essential that a conservative estimate be projected.
- The main concern is to account for expenses accurately and in as much detail as possible. This will then provide a target or breakeven figure toward which to work.
- Some headings may not be appropriate for your type of business; other headings should be added.
- see Figure 12

(c) Cash flow forecast
- A cash flow budget measures the flow of money in and out of the business. It is critical to you and your banker.
- Many businesses operate on a seasonal basis, as there are slow months and busy months. The cash flow budget projection will provide an indication of the times of a cash flow shortage to assist in properly planning and financing your operation. It will tell you in advance if you have enough cash to get by.
- A cash flow budget should be prepared a year in advance and contain monthly breakdowns.
- see Figure 13

(d) Cash flow assumptions
When reviewing the cash flow plan, certain assumptions should be made:
- Sales: monthly sales (consulting service fees) that are expected to materialise

Figure 10. *Continued*

- Receipts: cash sales represent cash actually received; debts collected represent the collection of amounts due for goods sold on credit; rental income is rent that will be collected in advance at the beginning of each month.
- Disbursements: accounts payable to be paid in the month following month of purchase.
- Accounting and legal: to be paid upon receipt of bill, expected to be in the spring or after your fiscal year end financial statements have been completed.
- Advertising: anticipated to be the same amount each month and paid for in the month the expense is incurred.
- Car: anticipated to be the same amount each month and paid for in the month the expense is incurred.
- Bank charges and interest: anticipated to be the same amount each month and paid for in the same month the expense is incurred.
- Equipment rental: to be paid for in monthly payments.
- Income tax: amount for tax of the prior year and to be paid in the spring.
- Insurance: annual premium to be paid quarterly, semi-annually or annually in equal instalments.
- Loan repayment: amount is the same each month and paid in accordance with the monthly schedule furnished by the lending institution.
- Office supplies and expenses: to be paid in month following receipt of invoice and supplies to be purchased on a quarterly basis.
- Licences: to be paid for upon due date.
- Telephone: to be paid for quarterly in month after receipt of bill. Amount expected to be the same each quarter.
- Utilities: expected to fluctuate with weather conditions and to be paid for quarterly.
- Wages and benefits: wages to increase after pay review. Amount otherwise considered to be the same each month and paid one month in arrears.
- Miscellaneous: expected to be the same each month and paid for in the same month the expense is incurred.
- Bad debts: variable.

Figure 10. *Continued*

(e) Break-even analysis
  — Your break-even analysis is a critical calculation for every business. Rather than calculating how much your firm would make if it attained an estimated sales volume, a more meaningful analysis determines at what sales volume your firm will break even. An estimated sales volume could be very unreliable as there are many factors which could affect revenue.
  — The calculation of a break-even point for every small business is one of the crucial pieces of information. Above the break-even sales volume it is only a matter of how much money your business can generate; below the break-even level of sales, it is only a matter of how many days a business can operate before bankruptcy.
  — A break-even analysis provides a very real and meaningful figure to work towards and might need updating every few months to reflect your business growth.
  — The break-even point is where total costs are equal to total revenues.
  — The calculation of total costs is determined by adding variable costs to the fixed costs.
  — Total costs are all costs of operating the business over a specified period.
  — Variable costs are those that vary directly with the number of services provided or marketing and promotion activities undertaken. These typically include car expenses, business travel expenses, supplies and brochures. Variable costs are not direct costs which are passed on to the client in the billing.
  — Fixed costs are costs that do not generally vary with the number of clients serviced. Also known as indirect costs, these costs typically include salaries, rent, secretarial service, insurance, telephone, accounting and legal supplies.

17. *Financing and capitalisation*
  (a) Term loan applied for
    — the amount, terms and when required
  (b) Purpose of term loan
    — attach a detailed description of the aspects of the business to be financed

Figure 10. *Continued*

    (c) Owner's equity
        — the amount of your financial commitment to the
           business
    (d) Summary of term loan requirements
        — for a particular project or for the business as a whole

18. *Operating loan*
    (a) Line of credit applied for
        — a new line of credit or an increase, and security offered
    (b) Maximum operating cash required
        — amount required, timing of need (refer to cash flow
           forecast)

19. *Present financing (if applicable)*
    (a) Term loans outstanding
        — the balance owing, repayment terms, purpose, security
           and status
    (b) Current operating line of credit
        — the amount and security held

20. *References*
    (a) Name of present lending institution
        — branch and type of accounts
    (b) Solicitor's name
        — address and telephone number
    (c) Accountant (name and practice name)
        — address and telephone number

21. *Appendix*
The nature of the contents of the appendices attached, if any,
depends on the circumstances and requirements of the lender
or investor, or the desire to enhance the loan proposal. It is
recommended that the appendices be prepared for your own
benefit and reference to assist your business analysis, and to be
available if the information is required. The following list is a
guide only. Some of the headings described may be unavailable
or unnecessary.
    (a) Personal net worth statement
        — includes personal property values, investments, cash,
           bank loans, credit accounts, mortgages and other
           liabilities. This will substantiate the value of your
           personal guarantee if required for security.
        — see Figure 14

Figure 10. *Continued*

  (b) Letter of intent
        – potential orders or client commitments
  (c) Description of personal and business insurance coverage
        – include insurance policies and amount of coverage
  (d) Summary of debtors
        – include ageing schedule of 30, 60 and 90 day periods
  (e) Summary of creditors
        – include schedule of payments and total amounts
          owing
  (f) Legal agreement
        – include a copy of contracts, leases and other
          documents
  (g) Appraisals
        – fair market value of business property and
          equipment
  (h) Financial statements for associated companies
        – where appropriate, a lender may require this
          information
  (i) References
  (j) Sales forecast and market surveys
  (k) List of investors
  (l) Credit status information
  (m) News articles about you and your business

---

2. Estimated need for business start-up cash

A detailed estimate of the start-up cash required should be calculated. Naturally, business situations can vary considerably.

During your first few months you will probably not have enough sales revenue to finance your short-term costs. This usually occurs for one of three reasons: your sales are below projection, your costs rise unexpectedly, or you have not yet been paid for work already performed. This last reason is called overdue debtors. Your conservative cash flow analysis prepares you for this situation, and enables you to plan your cash needs. If you are not paid on time, you cannot meet your costs. This is another reason why astute planning must be made with regard to credit and collection policies when dealing with customers. (See Figure 16.)

Figure 11. *Opening balance sheet*

	£ Cost	£ Depreciation	£ Net
Date			
Name of company			
FIXED ASSETS			
Land and buildings			
Plant and machinery			
Fixtures and fittings			
Motor vehicles			
Leasehold			
OTHER ASSETS			
TOTAL FIXED AND OTHER ASSETS		(A) £	
CURRENT ASSETS			
Stock and work-in-progress			
Debtors			
Prepayments			
Cash			
Bank			
TOTAL CURRENT ASSETS		(B) £	
TOTAL ASSETS (A+B) =		(C) £	
CURRENT LIABILITIES			
(amounts falling due within one year)			
Bank overdraft			
Loans			
Trade creditors			
Current portion of long-term debt			
Other current liabilities			
TOTAL CURRENT LIABILITIES		(D) £	
CURRENT LIABILITIES			
(amounts falling due after one year)			
Mortgages			
Loans from partners			
Other long-term loans			
TOTAL LONG-TERM DEBT		(E) £	
TOTAL LIABILITIES (D+E) =		(F) £	
Capital employed (C−F) =		(G) £	
Financed by:			
SHARE CAPITAL/PARTNERS' CAPITAL =		(G) £	

Figure 12.
Income and expense statement forecast

(Name of business)		
For the period: *months ending* *, 19*		
PROJECTED INCOME		£
SALES		
TOTAL SALES		
OTHER INCOME		
TOTAL INCOME	(A)	£
PROJECTED EXPENSES		

Sales expenses
    Commissions and salaries
    Travel
    Advertising
    Motor expenses
    Other		

TOTAL SELLING EXPENSES	(B)	£

ADMINISTRATIVE AND FINANCIAL EXPENSES
    Management salaries (or proprietor/partner draws)
    Office salaries
    Professional fees (eg accountant's fees)
    Office expenses and supplies
    Telephone
    Rent
    Interest and bank charges
    Stock depreciation
    Bad debt
    Other		

TOTAL ADMINISTRATIVE AND FINANCIAL EXPENSES	(C)	£
TOTAL EXPENSES (B+C) =	(D)	£

OPERATING PROFIT (LOSS) (A–D)
    Add: Other income
    Less: Provisions for income taxes
		£

NET PROFIT (LOSS)		£

Figure 13. *Cash flow forecast*

	January		February		March	
	Est	Actual	Est	Actual	Est	Actual
Cash at beginning of month:	£	£	£	£	£	£
In bank and on hand						
In investments						
TOTAL CASH	£	£	£	£	£	£
Plus income during month:						
Cash sales (include credit cards)						
Credit sales payments						
Investment income						
Debtors						
Loans						
Personal investment						
Other cash income						
TOTAL CASH AND INCOME	£	£	£	£	£	£
Expenses during the month:						
Rent (if applicable)						
Electricity						
Gas						
Phone						
Postage						
Office equipment and furniture						
Stationery and business cards						
Insurance (business, fire, liability, theft, fire etc)						
Answering service						

Figure 13. *Continued*

Printing and supplies					
Typing/secretarial service					
Accounting and legal services					
Advertising and promotion					
Business licences and permits					
Dues and subscriptions					
Books and reference materials					
Travel: UK					
Travel: Abroad					
Conventions, professional meetings, trade shows					
Continuing education					
Entertainment					
Contributions					
Gifts					
Salaries					
National Insurance					
Taxation					
Pensions					
Miscellaneous					
Loan repayment					
Other cash expenses					
TOTAL EXPENSES	£	£	£	£	£
Cash flow or deficit at end of month	£	£	£	£	£
Cash flow cumulative (monthly)	£	£	£	£	£

For convenience, value added tax is omitted from these calculations.

Figure 14. *Personal net worth statement*

Date:

Name:

Address:

GENERAL INFORMATION

Home phone: Age: Married or single:

Business phone: Dependents (including spouse):

Present employer:

How long with this employer?

Position occupied:

Previous employer: How long?

Monthly mortgage repayment:

Home address:

Salary, wages, or commission per annum: £

Other income: £   Source:

Guarantees on debts of others: £   Name:

ASSETS

Bank accounts:

Shares at cost (market value:)

Bonds at cost (market value:)

Life assurance (cash surrender value):

   Beneficiary:

Motor vehicle value:

   Year: Make:

Figure 14. *Continued*

Home value:

Building size:

Other assets:

TOTAL ASSETS   (A) £

LIABILITIES

Bank loans:

Credit cards (Visa, Access, American Express, Diners Club):

Charge accounts (department stores):

Loans on life assurance policy:

Other loans (personal etc):

Hire purchase (total car or furniture):

Mortgages:

   Interest rate: Term: Payments:

Total mortgage debt outstanding:

Other liabilities:

TOTAL LIABILITIES   (B) £

NET WORTH (A—B) =   (C) £

Figure 15. *Personal monthly expense checklist*

Budget for the month of			
Item	**Budget**	**Actual**	**Variance**
Food	£	£	£
Housing:			
Monthly payment			
Rates (if owned)			
Insurance			
Clothing			
Car:			
Payment			
Petrol			
Repairs			
Insurance			
Utilities:			
Electricity			
Gas			
Telephone			
Water rates			
Personal spending (gifts)			
Credit cards (not covered elsewhere)			
Instalment and other loans			
Life assurance			
Taxation			
Recreation			
Travel			
Investment, including saving			
Donations			
Medical insurance			
Education (family)			
Miscellaneous			
TOTALS	£	£	£

Figure 16. *Start-up costs worksheet*

Item	Estimated monthly expenses £	Estimated start-up expense £
Owner/manager salary	x 2 =	
Other salaries and wages	x 3 =	
Rent	x 3 =	
Advertising	x 3 =	
Delivery expenses	x 3 =	
Supplies	x 3 =	
Telephone	x 3 =	
Electricity	x 3 =	
Gas	x 3 =	
Insurance	x 3 =	
Taxation	x 3 =	
National Insurance contributions	x 4 =	
Interest	x 3 =	
Maintenance	x 3 =	
Legal and professional fees	x 3 =	
Other	x 3 =	
Fixture and equipment purchase		
Decorating and remodelling		
Installation of fixtures and equipment		
Opening stock		
Licences and permits		
Utilities connection charges		
Pre-opening advertising and promotion		
Cash for unexpected expenses		
TOTAL		£

Note. For some businesses, you may have to multiply your estimated monthly expenses by a larger factor than shown here. For example, if you plan to open a seasonal business, you may want a cash reserve to cover six months of operating expenses.

Summary

Before presenting your business plan to a lender or investor, have two or three impartial outsiders review the finished plan in detail. There may be something you have overlooked or under-emphasised. After your plan has been reviewed by others, take your plan and financial statements to your accountant for review. You and your accountant should also discuss all the personal and business tax considerations that might be involved. You may wish your accountant to accompany you to the bank when you discuss your loan proposal. This is not uncommon and can create a very positive impression.

Discuss the plan with your solicitor regarding the security that you are proposing. Before the plan is submitted, your solicitor should explain fully the effect of your pledging collateral security and what the lender could do if you default. You should also seriously evaluate if the security pledged is too excessive for the loan or risk involved, or if the risk is too great for the exposure of pledging your personal assets.

Your familiarity with the business plan will increase your credibility and at the same time provide you with a good understanding of what the financial statements reveal about the viability of your business.

Chapter 13

Reasons for Business Failure and Success

Reasons for failure

Statistics vary, but approximately 80 per cent of small businesses fail within the first three years of starting up. There are many reasons for this. Studies show that the entrepreneur's personal limitations are the primary reason. This includes, in order of priority, lack of personal qualifications to run a business, lack of experience in the line of business, lack of training, and unbalanced experience. These limitations lead to the following more specific reasons:

1. Failure to self-evaluate realistically

Failure to make a frank assessment of your strengths and weaknesses, needs and desires is a common mistake. Obtain objective feedback from friends, relatives, family or business associates.

2. Failure to set goals

No goals or objectives are made, and if they are, they are ineffective because they are not specific, measurable, or realistic. Preparing a business plan is an integral part of goal setting.

3. Failure to revise goals

If goals are set, failure to reassess them can cause problems. As the business plan is implemented, new uncertainties can affect it, such as the loss of key personnel, illness of owners, over-ambitious timetables, new competition, increase in lending rates and supplier problems. Reassessment of your goal is only practical and realistic.

4. Failure to anticipate obstacles

Excessive optimism can seriously impede an attitude of identifying potential obstacles and planning solutions to overcome them.

5. Failure to set progress targets and reviews

Failure to set specific milestones and dates to review them, or else ignoring the review dates, can lead to business troubles. Periodic reviews alert you to a need for reassessment. Reviewing the targets you have met can provide an important sense of accomplishment, and motivate you to carry on.

6. Lack of commitment

Personal commitment is critical to the success of any business plan. It provides the motivation to see the goal through to completion. But unless the people who must implement the business plan are committed to it, the business will fail. That is why it is important to select employees, partners, management team members, and professional advisers very carefully. Collaboration helps to arrive at jointly established goals.

7. Failure to learn from experience

An inflexible attitude can cause bad judgements to be repeated.

8. Failure to obtain sufficient capital

Under-capitalisation is a common problem. Owners typically overestimate the revenue and underestimate the costs and length of time needed to get established. Businesses simply run out of money before they are able to generate their own funds. An integral part of this problem is lack of back-up capital to deal with unforeseen circumstances. Under-capitalisation may come from lack of experience or knowledge or from poor planning.

Reasons for success

By now you probably have a good idea of the factors that

contribute to entrepreneurial success. Reflect on the reasons for failure described above and set out to do the opposite. Review the chapter on the characteristics of successful entrepreneurs and your personal assessment, then ask yourself how close you are. Make sure you complete all the quizzes and exercises as best you can. Attempt to follow the tips outlined throughout this book and avoid the classic pitfalls of small business people. Seek and obtain quality input from your professional advisers and from those people who matter most. Be honest with yourself.

There are many other ways to help you to achieve business success. Learn about philosophies and techniques for personal success, motivation, goal setting and time management through books, magazines and seminars. Read about people who have been successful, and where you can, cultivate acquaintance with successful entrepreneurs, to use as role models. Study how they work and try to learn from them.

The fact that you have gone through this book in detail, with all the work involved, demonstrates your perseverance, discipline, and desire for knowledge. These are all integral facets of achieving success as an entrepreneur. Your desire to read this book shows that you want to achieve success. The dream is the first step to achieving the reality.

Best wishes on your future entrepreneurial success and endeavours.

Appendices

Business Publications

Many business publications, issued by government departments and professional practices, are free; the most useful are
described in *Sources of Free Business Information*, published
by Kogan Page.

The following loose-leaf publications are available from
Croner Publications Ltd, Croner House, 173 Kingston Road,
New Malden, Surrey KT3 3SS:

> *Buying and Selling Law*
> *Guide to Corporation Tax*
> *Management Information Manual*
> *Reference Book for the Self-Employed and Small Business*
> *Reference Book for VAT.*

Kogan Page publish an extensive list of books for small and
medium-sized businesses; those particularly helpful to the
reader of this book are likely to be:

Be Your Own Company Secretary, A J Scrine, 1987
The Business Fact Finder, editor Hano Johannsen, 1987
Buying a Shop, 3rd edition, A St John Price, 1986
Choosing and Using Professional Advisers,
    editor Paul Chaplin, 1986
Don't Do. Delegate! James M Jenks and John M Kelly, 1986
*Effective Advertising: The Daily Telegraph Guide for the
    Small Business*, H C Carter, 1986
Export for the Small Business, Henry Deschampsneufs, 1984
Finance and Accounts for Managers, Desmond Goch, 1986
Financial Management for the Small Business, Colin Barrow,
    1984
*Getting Sales: A Practical Guide to Getting More Sales for
    Your Business*, R D Smith and G M Dick, 1986
How to be a Better Manager, Michael Armstrong, 1983

How to Buy a Business: The Daily Telegraph Guide,
   Peter Farrell, 1983

*How to Choose Business Premises: A Guide for the Small
   Firm*, Howard Green, Brian Chalkley and Paul Foley,
   1986

*Importing for the Small Business: The Daily Telegraph
   Guide*, Mag Morris, 1985

Law for the Small Business: The Daily Telegraph Guide,
   5th edition, Patricia Clayton, 1987

A Manager's Guide to Patents, Trade Marks and Copyright,
   John F Williams, 1986

The Practice of Successful Business Management,
   Kenneth Winckles, 1986

Raising Finance: The Guardian Guide for the Small Business,
   2nd edition, Clive Woodcock, 1985

So You Think Your Business Needs a Computer?
   Khalid Aziz, 1986

Starting a Successful Small Business, M J Morris, 1985

*Successful Expansion for the Small Business: The Daily
   Telegraph Guide*, M J Morris, 1985

*Successful Marketing for the Small Business: The Daily
   Telegraph Guide*, Dave Patten, 1985

Taking Up a Franchise: The Daily Telegraph Guide,
   3rd edition, Godfrey Golzen and Colin Barrow, 1986

*Which Business? How to Select the Right Opportunity for
   Starting Up*, Stephen Halliday, 1987

Winning Strategies for Managing People, Robert Irwin and
   Rita Wolenik, 1986

*Working for Yourself: The Daily Telegraph Guide to
   Self-Employment*, 9th edition, Godfrey Golzen, 1987

Buying a Business

This checklist provides the general questions you should ask before buying an existing business. It does not contain all the questions pertaining to a specific business opportunity. If you want more information, see *How to Buy a Business*, another title published by Kogan Page.

Sales

- Is the product or service likely to maintain or improve its marketability, or is it in danger of becoming oversold, out of style, or obsolete?
- Is the business in a good location or is poor location the reason it is for sale?
- Are prices competitive? Are competitors gaining strength?
- Are all sales documented in reliable records? Are the total sales broken down by product line, if applicable?
- Are bad debts deducted from sales, or are they still shown as debtors?
- What is the sales pattern year by year and month by month? Is the pattern seasonal or related to some business cycle, such as home construction or another uncontrollable variable?
- Are some goods sold on consignment with the right of being returned for full credit?
- Are some goods under guarantee or warranty?
- Are some fluctuations in sales due to lucky one-shot sales?
- Is a particular salesperson, or the seller, critical to success?

- Are you sure all sales are for this business, and that the seller hasn't added sales from another business?
- Will you be able to continue buying the product from existing suppliers?
- Can you increase sales with current resources?

Costs

- Are all expenses shown?
- Is there a chance the owner has paid expenses through another business?
- Has the owner avoided some expenses that could be delayed such as equipment maintenance?
- Are there annual expenses coming due soon?
- Are there new or increased expenses you should anticipate?
- Is an adequate salary allowed for work done by the owner and his or her family?
- Is interest paid for money lent to the business?
- Is depreciation claimed for the equipment and, if so, is it reasonable, particularly for the price you'll be paying?
- Are the staff adequately paid, or do they expect increases soon?
- Does your lease have an escalation clause to include increases in management costs, such as light, heat and so on? When will it have to be renegotiated?
- What effect would decreased or increased sales have on your costs?
- What expenses do similar businesses have?
- Do you know what costs are allocated to which product, and how a change in your product mix would affect costs?
- Are some expenses prepaid by the seller? Will you have to reimburse the seller for your share?
- Has the stock been accurately shown at true current value, for calculating actual cost of goods sold?

Profits

- Have you looked at the effect on profit of increased or decreased sales?

- Do you know the likely minimum and maximum sales?
- Have you considered what effect inflation will have over the years to come? On sales? On costs?
- Are profits adequate to warrant the risk?
  Have you analysed the financial records for the last three years including balance sheets, profit and loss accounts, tax returns, purchases and sales records and bank statements? Have the records been well kept? Have they been verified by a qualified accountant?
- Based on past financial results, have you projected the future cash flow and profitability of the business? What is the break-even point?

Assets

- Do you know exactly what you are buying and not buying? Are there lists and have you checked them?
- What is the market value and replacement value of the fixed assets?
- If stock or work-in-progress is to be included, has a value been agreed upon at the time of offer? Have you agreed on how it will be adjusted at time of closing, and within what limits?
- Has any stock been sold but not despatched?
- Have you decided what extras you want — mailing lists, business name, exclusive rights, leases etc? Can they be transferred?
- If you need new licences, do you know what is required to get them?
- Are you buying the outstanding debtors? Do you have a listing of these accounts by age?
- What could you sell the debtors for to a factoring agency?
- Is equipment in good repair? Is it efficient? Is it in danger of becoming obsolete or difficult to service? Could it be sold easily?
- Is any equipment leased? Do you know the terms and the cost of each lease? Will you get ownership on maturity?
- Will you have to build up your own debtors? Have you worked out how this will affect your cash flow?

- If the business is a limited company, are you buying the shares or the assets? Be sure to consult a solicitor and tax accountant on this point as there are advantages and disadvantages.
- Have you consulted a qualified accountant on how to value the various assets for the best tax advantage? How are you allocating the value for goodwill? Is it realistic?

Liabilities

- Are the assets you're buying free of debts and liens? Have you checked this carefully? If you are assuming some debts, do you know the exact terms of repayment? Is this in writing?
- Are there any contingencies, such as warranties or guaranteed debts or accounts? Are you assuming any risk of being liable for the previous owner's actions (as might happen when buying the shares of a limited company)? Will your customers expect you to make refunds or warranties whether or not you're legally obliged to, risking their goodwill?
- Has the previous owner received any payments in advance (eg deposits) that he or she should turn over to you?
- Have you checked the business's credit rating with suppliers? Will you receive an established rating or be treated as a new account?
- If buying part of a company or entering a partnership, do you know what limits there are on one person making a commitment on behalf of the business?
- Do you know the effect the build-up of your bought ledger will have on your cash flow?
- Will your cash flow from operations be enough to pay your debts?

The seller and you

- Do you know the real reason why the business is for sale? How have you satisfied yourself as to what the true facts are?

- Is the seller being cooperative in supplying you with information?
- Is the seller willing to sign a non-competition agreement?
- Will the seller train you and assist you after the purchase?
- Is this the type of business you were actually looking for?
- Is the type and size of business compatible with your interests, experience, personality and capital?

The purchase agreement

- Does the draft agreement cover what assets are to be purchased, what liabilities are to be assumed and when the business is to be taken over?
- Are you ready to negotiate? Remember, a business is worth no more than the highest price someone will pay and no less than the lowest price the seller will accept.
- In drafting your offer, have you included escape clauses covering obtaining financing, inspecting all records, receiving necessary licences and rights, other transfers?
- Have you obtained legal and qualified accounting and tax advice before submitting an offer?

Evaluating a Franchise

This checklist provides the general questions you should ask before committing yourself to a franchise business. It does not contain all the questions pertaining to a specific franchise. For more information see *Taking up a Franchise: The Daily Telegraph Guide*, published by Kogan Page (3rd edition, 1986).

Company history and reputation

- How long has the franchisor been in operation?
- Is the franchisor a member of the British Franchise Association?
- If the franchisor is a new firm, how long has the concept been tested? What are the results?
- What is the firm's record of accomplishment?
- Does the firm have a reputation for honesty with its franchisees? With its customers?
- Who are the principals of the firm?
- In what regard are these principals held in the business community?
- What experience have the principals of the firm had in this type of business?
- Is the firm adequately financed? Have you seen a recent financial statement?
- What are the plans for future development and expansion?
- What effect will development and expansion have on your dealings with the firm?
- How does the firm stand with the chamber of commerce or Dun and Bradstreet?

- How selective is the company in choosing its franchisees? Did they ask your qualifications?

The franchise product or service

- How would you evaluate the product or service's quality?
- Would you buy the product or service on its own merit?
- Are you prepared to spend the remainder of your business life with this product or service?
- Will this product or service sell year-round in your area or are you going to be out of business for some months of the year? Would you be prepared for a slack period?
- Will this product or service increase in demand or is it a passing fad?
- Is the product or service priced competitively with others in its class?
- Is it packaged well and will the packaging help to promote sales?
- How long has this product or service been on the market in its present form?
- Where is the product or service now sold and what guarantee do you have that it will sell in your area?

The franchised sales area

- How well defined is the franchise sales area? Is it outlined on a map? In the contract?
- Do you have the exclusive right to the franchise in this area?
- What is the sales potential of the territory? Population? Income?
- What has the growth of the territory been?
- What is the future growth potential?
- What type of people are moving into the territory? Their income?
- Is the territory's population homogeneous? That is, is it made up of the same or different groups of people? Is this good or bad for your product or service?
- How much direct competition for your type of product or service is currently in this area?

- How much competition for sales by value can be expected in the territory? From other franchises? From non-franchised business?
- Are the existing competitive franchises in the territory successful?

The franchise contract

- Does the contract fully explain the franchise agreement as you understand it?
- Did your solicitor approve the contract after he or she studied it in detail?
- Does the contract benefit both parties?
- Are you able to terminate the contract if, for some reason, you have to?
- What would it cost you if you have to terminate the contract?
- Can you sell the contract with the franchisor's consent? And can you keep profits made from the sale?
- Can the franchisor take back or terminate the contract at his or her option? Under what conditions?
- If the franchisor terminates the contract, will you be compensated for goodwill you have built up in the business?
- Does the contract specify the type and size of operation?
- Are your payments to the franchisor spelled out in detail?
- Must a certain amount of merchandise be purchased from the franchisor?
- Can you use your own suppliers?
- Must you meet a certain yearly sales quota? Is it attainable?
- Are you prevented from engaging in any other business activity for the duration of the contract?
- Does the contract prevent you from establishing, owning or working in a competing business for a certain number of years after termination?
- Before you sign the sales contract, are you sure that the franchise can do something for you that you cannot do for yourself?

Franchisor's assistance to you

- Does the franchisor provide continuing assistance? Is it specified in the contract?
- Are you and your key personnel required to go to a special training school? Is the school of sufficient calibre to teach you the necessary methods? Who pays?
- Have you seen and examined the company's franchise manual, the accounting system, and all other systems and methods to which you will have to adhere?
- Does the franchisor select the business site? Is there a fee? Can you refuse the site? Can you choose your own site?
- Will the franchisor give you help on the lease agreement? Is it in the contract?
- Will the franchisor assist with an opening stock? Purchasing? Stock control?
- Will the franchisor help with the financing arrangements? At what cost to you?
- What advertising and sales promotion assistance is provided? What is your cost for this assistance?
- If a well known personality is involved, does he or she assist you directly? How?
- Will the franchisor provide legal assistance?
- Does the franchisor design the store layouts and displays? Will this layout fit into your territory?
- Have you spoken to other franchisees? How many?

Useful Addresses

Advisory, Conciliation and
Arbitration Service (ACAS)
Head Office
11-12 St James's Square
London SW1Y 4LA
01-214 3600
and Regional offices

Alliance of Small Firms and
Self-Employed People Ltd
42 Vine Road
East Molesey
Surrey KT8 9LF
01-979 2293

Association of British Chambers
of Commerce
212a Shaftesbury Avenue
London WC2H 8EW
01-240 5831

Association of British Factors Ltd
Moor House
London Wall
London EC2Y 5HE
01-638 4090

Association of Invoice Factors
Jordan House
London Wall
London EC2Y 5HE
01-638 4090

British Franchise Association
75a Bell Street
Henley-on-Thames
Oxon RG9 2BD
0491 578049

British Insurance Brokers'
Association
14 Bevis Marks
London EC3A 7NT
01-623 9043

British Overseas Trade Board
1 Victoria Street
London SW1H 0ET
01-215 7877

Chartered Institute of
Patent Agents
Staple Inn Buildings
335 High Holborn
London WC1V 7PX
01-405 9450

Collection Agencies Association
5 Mill Street
Bedford MK40 3EU
0234 4566

Companies Registration Office
Companies House
55 City Road
London EC1Y 1BB
01-253 9393

102 George Street
Edinburgh EH2 3JD
031-225 5774

Chichester House
43-47 Chichester Court
Belfast BT1 4PJ
0232 234121

Co-operative Development Agency
21 Panton Street
London SW1Y 4DR
01-839 2988

Council for Small Industries in
Rural Areas (CoSIRA)
141 Castle Street
Salisbury
Wilts SP1 3TP
0722 336255
and Regional offices

Equipment Leasing Association
18 Upper Grosvenor Street
London W1X 9PB
01-491 2783

Finance Houses Association
18 Upper Grosvenor Street
London W1X 9PB
01-491 2783

Highlands and Islands
Development Board
Bridge House
Bank Street
Inverness IV1 1QR
0463 34171

Investors in Industry
(formerly ICFC)
Head Office
91 Waterloo Road
London SE1 8XP
01-928 7822

Law Society
113 Chancery Lane
London WC2A 1PL
01-242 1222

London Enterprise Agency
4 Snow Hill
London EC1A 2BS
01-236 3000

Manufacturing Advisory Service
(MAS)
Production Engineering Research
Association
Melton Mowbray
Leicestershire LE13 0PB
0664 64133

Mid Wales Development Board
Ladywell House
Newtown
Powys SY16 1JB
0686 26965

National Computing Centre Ltd
Oxford Road
Manchester M1 7ED
061-228 6333

National Federation of Self-
Employed and Small Business Ltd
32 St Anne's Road West
Lytham St Anne's
Lancashire FY8 1NY
0253 720911

Northern Ireland Development
Agency
100 Belfast Road
Holywood
County Down
Northern Ireland
02317 4232

Patent Office (includes Trade
Marks Registry and
Designs Registry)
State House
66-71 High Holborn
London WC1R 4TP
01-831 2525

The Registrar of Companies
Companies House
Crown Way
Maindy
Cardiff CF4 3UZ
0222 388588

The Scottish Development
Agency
(Small Business Division)
102 Telford Road
Edinburgh EH4 2NP
031-343 1911

Small Firms Service
Department of Employment
Ring the operator on 100 and ask
for Freefone Enterprise. You will
be put in touch with your nearest
regional office

Venture Capital Reports
The Refuge Building
20 Baldwin Street
Bristol BS1 1SE
0272 272250

Index